T0209700

FROM YOUR MAT TO YOUR MEMOIR

*Creating a Yogic Writing Practice to
Find and Write Your Life Stories*

REBECCA LYN GOLD

BALBOA.PRESS
A DIVISION OF HAY HOUSE

Balboa Press books may be ordered through booksellers or by contacting:

Balboa Press
A Division of Hay House
1663 Liberty Drive
Bloomington, IN 47403
www.balboapress.com
844-682-1282

Because of the dynamic nature of the Internet, any web addresses or links contained in this book may have changed since publication and may no longer be valid. The views expressed in this work are solely those of the author and do not necessarily reflect the views of the publisher, and the publisher hereby disclaims any responsibility for them.

The author of this book does not dispense medical advice or prescribe the use of any technique as a form of treatment for physical, emotional, or medical problems without the advice of a physician, either directly or indirectly. The intent of the author is only to offer information of a general nature to help you in your quest for emotional and spiritual well-being. In the event you use any of the information in this book for yourself, which is your constitutional right, the author and the publisher assume no responsibility for your actions.

Any people depicted in stock imagery provided by Getty Images are models, and such images are being used for illustrative purposes only. Certain stock imagery © Getty Images.

Print information available on the last page.

ISBN: 979-8-7652-4579-8 (sc)
ISBN: 979-8-7652-4580-4 (hc)
ISBN: 979-8-7652-4581-1 (e)

Library of Congress Control Number: 2023918432

Balboa Press rev. date: 11/20/2023

"Mom, you *HAVE* to go to yoga."
This book is for you, Nisha, because I did.

~

ACKNOWLEDGMENTS

I would like to extend my deepest gratitude for my Prannothan Yoga teachers and family, especially Devarshi Steven Hartman, Joan Dwyer, Mel Wegimont, Kendall Sheldon, Lisa Dahl, Alice Braunstein, and Tara Beauleau.

Yin Goddesses: Alicia Barry, Jenn Thomas, and Amy Jones.

Amy Weintraub, whose book "Yoga For Depression" landed in my hands at the *write* time.

My writing teachers and mentors, including: Dani Shapiro, Natalie Goldberg, Julia Cameron, Lesléa Newman, Candace Walsh, Tanya Taylor Rubenstein, and most especially, Uncle Greg.

My sister Pamela Sardinha for the photos of my dear friend Sharon Gentile Penta.

Kim Fuller for the cover photo of my beautiful friend Cindy Arrighi. Her memory will be with me always.

And finally, to Osvaldo, for your unwavering love and support and (always!) finding my typos.

CONTENTS

TWENTY-ONE DAY WRITING JOURNEY

INTRODUCTION

"There is no greater agony than bearing
an untold story inside you."
—Zora Neale Hurston

I love this quote, and I agree wholeheartedly. Yet sometimes we want to write our stories and find we can't. The words might be swirling around our minds but resist being captured on the page. Or when we sit down to write, anxiety mounts and all we hear is an internal voice that says something like: *You have no idea what you're doing, so don't even start.* Or, best-case scenario, we have pages of notes or even full drafts, but when we look back at what we've written, the writing feels boring and unemotional. The facts are there, but the heart and soul are missing.

Spoiler alert: I've been there. But the good news is there is a way out.

When we encounter obstacles in our writing, it's easy to assume the problem is all in our heads. But yoga philosophy teaches us that nothing is all in our heads, in large part because our minds are just one layer through which we experience our world and hold our stories. Along with our mind, our physical body, energetic body, intuition, and soul are all parts of our whole being. Our life stories (especially those that may be traumatic) are stored in all these layers. We need to make space for the stories to reveal themselves before we sit down to write. But how do we do that?

I remember one day a few years ago I announced to my kids: "I'm gonna run a marathon!"

They cracked up. Seriously, laughed so hard it made me furious. "Mom, you don't just wake up one day and run a marathon," my pragmatic son told me. "You have to train and practice for years!"

You know what? He was right. And you know what else? I didn't train or practice, and I've yet to run a marathon.

But what I have been practicing (*for years!*) is writing.

I've been training myself every morning to sit down for thirty minutes that include: ten minutes of yoga, five minutes of pranayama (breathwork), five minutes of meditation, and ten minutes of writing. This is what I call my *yogic writing practice.*

So why do I do all that? Why not just open my journal and write?

Yoga brings me in touch with my physical body. Pranayama (breath practice) brings awareness to what keeps me alive in the moment. Meditation brings awareness to my thoughts and deep wisdom. Then putting pen to paper allows me to blend all that energy together and write from a place of wholeness and truth.

Now, in all honesty, some days I don't do each step—I might just do the breath practice, or the meditation, or the yoga poses before my ten minutes of writing. But regardless of which mind/body practice I choose before I write, I allow whatever comes out in my practice to just "be." With my poses, my breath, my meditation, my words... I surrender wholeheartedly to whatever shows up on my mat—and on the page—without judgment. This is where I get to be me: the messy, klutzy, monkey-brain, imperfect writer that I am. And what shows up is different every day.

At another time during the day (sometimes right after) I sit for a longer writing session and work on whatever story or writing project I am in the middle of. Perhaps something came up during my practice that I want to explore further and craft into a story. Maybe I'm writing a new chapter to a book or an essay for a blog, or maybe I'll work on something I've been playing with all week, or month, or year!

The point is, I don't just jump into writing a book; just like I don't just go outside and run a marathon (or a mile, for that matter). I think of writing in two parts: *practice* and *product*. I first do my practice and then work on my product. They are two separate things.

Writing is like a muscle. You have to use it over and over again in order for it to be better and stronger. A daily yogic writing practice can be your training ground. So, when you sit down to work on your *product* (your memoir, for example) even if it's once a week or once a month, your muscle memory kicks into gear *(Oh, we're writing again! I remember this! Fun!)*, and you're able to dive into your writing more quickly and with less resistance. You gave the resistance and the inner critic space to show up during your practice, so now they've left the building.

WARNING: When you start writing your memoir or any other book, you will be tempted to give up your writing practice. Your mind will start to tell you things like, *That fifteen minutes is a waste of time. You've only got an hour— better to use that time writing your book.*

This is sabotage! You still need to keep up your practice even if you're midway through writing the greatest American novel. A marathon runner still needs to stretch before every single run. A yogic writing practice reunites your body, mind, internal wisdom, and intuition with pen and paper. It's the stretch your writer self needs. Don't give up your practice for your product.

I like to say that we write to heal, we write to reveal, and we write to leave our legacy. Your yogic writing **practice** is for healing and revealing. Your **product** is your legacy.

That is what brings me to this book—those stories that are swirling around in your mind but resist being captured on the page, or those words that are on the page but read like an emotionless guidebook, or those life moments that you haven't been able to remember let alone write about... You can say goodbye to all of that.

I want to share this path I have found from my mat to my memoir. I want you to experience the healing power of yogic writing so that you too can write your life stories and leave your legacy.

This book unfolds in two parts:

Part I: About Yogic Writing. An introduction to the "pancha kosha" theory in yogic philosophy: the five layers of awareness through which we experience life. Each chapter balances the philosophy alongside practices on how to bring awareness to each layer. When you bring awareness to these layers, memories are recovered, and stories are revealed.

Part II: Find and Write Your Life Stories. This is a Twenty-one-day journey that includes yogic practices and writing prompts to find and write your life stories. You will be introduced to yoga poses to open areas of the body where trauma or memories may be stored, breath control practices to stimulate and balance the brain, and meditations with mudras and mantras to gain insight and inspiration.

Each practice is accompanied by a juicy writing prompt to tap into the subconscious; uncover memories; and write deep, authentic life stories. At the end of the journey, you will have written twenty-one stories to jumpstart your memoir. More importantly, you will have created a sustainable writing practice that will lead you down the path—from your mat to your memoir.

You will also have access to a community of writers who are also taking (or who have taken) this twenty-one-day yogic writing journey on a private Facebook group to share your thoughts and stories. I'll see you there!

BEFORE YOU GO ANY FURTHER—hear me out. When I google a recipe and it forces me to read a whole lot of (what I deem) unimportant stuff about the food I'm about to prepare, I get bored and impatient. I just want the ingredients and the steps to cook the dish! Or when I buy a diet book and the first part is scientific evidence about why other diets don't work and this one will... but really all I want is the daily food plan. Well, suffice it to say that I've kind of done the same thing with this book. So, if you're interested in why and how this practice works, then read Section 1. But if you just want to jump to the *daily food plan,* go right to Section 2 and start writing!

CHAPTER 1

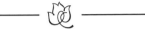

My Story: From the Meds to the Mat to the Memoir

In the early 1990s, I thought I'd struck gold. In fact, I had. I'd married a man with the last name Gold! Together, with my 9-year-old daughter, we had moved to South America and back again, adopting a baby in the process. And after spending nearly a decade in the personal computer industry teaching and writing training manuals, I had finally found a way to sustain myself doing what I loved—creative writing.

I'd leveraged my expertise in computers to write a biography about Steve Wozniak, *A Wizard Called Woz,* one of the founders of Apple. I wrote and edited stories from expectant adoptive parents, which then became my next book, *Till There Was You: An Adoption Expectancy Journal.* I was becoming widely published in magazines and websites, including a syndicated column in a well-known parenting magazine. I had a contract in hand with a large publishing house for a children's nonfiction book about human rights, a topic I'd been deeply interested in since living in Argentina. I started to dabble in young-adult fiction and was getting positive responses from agents and editors. And I became pregnant and gave birth to our son.

Life was good. No, life was *great.* I was happily married to a wonderful man and living in beautiful southern California. I had three amazing children, a teaching job I loved, and a budding writing career.

And then something else showed up, unannounced.

That something was depression.

I wasn't just having a bad day or week, but rather a return visit from the debilitating, near-suicidal depression I had suffered in my teens. I was, on the outside, happy and healthier than I had ever been, but damn if that heaviness in my shoulder didn't start to make me slump, causing me to walk a little slower and smile less and less every day. I was unable to feel joy. I could barely get out of bed, and when I did, all I wanted to do was crawl back in. I didn't want to be with anyone, including my husband, friends, or even my children. I stopped writing, publishing, or even wanting to write. I gave up all of my in-progress work.

"Mom, you *have* to go to yoga," my teenage daughter began to campaign.

"Been there, done that," I said. "No, thanks."

What my daughter didn't know was that I'd had an experience with what I *thought* was yoga in my early twenties and convinced myself it was not for me. At the time, I had dropped out of college, driven across the country from Vermont to California, and taken a job waitressing the graveyard shift at a coffee shop. I spent a lot of time wandering through my days, and one day I'd moseyed into a building with a "Yoga and Meditation Center" sign on the door. In 1980, a sign like that wasn't commonplace.

I walked into a room full of men and women dressed in white from head to toe. They were sitting cross-legged on floor cushions, chanting. A young man got up and started to lead me into the room and told me to take a seat. He told me to close my eyes and breathe. "Your life will change," he said.

I stiffened immediately. His words recalled a traumatic experience I'd had in my early teens when I was recruited by a leader in Adidam, one of the many cults that sprang up in the early 1970s. At fourteen, I had spent several months with a group of latchkey and troubled teens like myself in a home led by a false prophet posing as a guitar teacher, whose self-proclaimed calling was to change our lives and heal our souls. All we had to do was exactly what he told us to do, without question.

His chosen methodologies were drugs, sex, secrets and mind games, in between sessions of chanting and supposed "music lessons." It took me nearly a year to break free from his teachings, and the experience left me with a deep-rooted cynicism toward anyone claiming to be a guru preaching a better way to live.

The yoga center in Long Beach brought me back to those days, and I was frightened. I turned around and walked out of the building as fast as I could. Yoga, I decided right then and there, was *not* for me.

But now, nearly 2 decades later, my daughter insisted. She told me she found an awesome yoga teacher at a nearby gym. Because she kept insisting, I went and watched beautiful young bodies doing handstands and headstands and moving in all sorts of positions with ease, while I could barely touch my toes. I loved watching my daughter with her newfound passion, but once again, I was convinced that yoga was not in my cards.

Eventually, with the help of a therapist and medication, I found my way back to my life, although not back to my writing. That book, so to speak, was closed and put way back on the shelf.

Fast forward ten years. We moved from California to Rhode Island. My kids were becoming more independent (aka needing me less), and out of nowhere, my desire to write and publish came back with a vengeance. But every time I sat down to write, stories from my past would sneak up to the page. Every time that happened, I quickly closed my journal or computer. I did *not* want to go there, to write about moments in my life that weren't happy ones.

Instead, I tried to write stories for children and feel-good stories about family life, like I'd published in years past, but my writing felt stale, unimportant, uninspiring. It hadn't occurred to me that I was now living in the town where I grew up, where the trauma of my teenage years had taken place. Clearly, it was time for me to write my own life stories. But I couldn't get past the first sentence or two.

What could possibly help?

I heard that Natalie Goldberg was hosting a writer's retreat at Kripalu Center for Yoga and Health, which was a few hours away from where I lived. I had long ago devoured her book *Writing Down the Bones* and was intrigued with the idea of writing practice. I thought that might be just what I needed to get unstuck. But the catch was it was held at a *yoga* retreat center! Why was yoga constantly trying to make its way into my life?

Natalie urged us to try the different yoga and meditation offerings at Kripalu while we were there, so I did. And for the first time I thought yoga was *kind of interesting*. And maybe, just maybe, it wasn't as weird or as difficult as I had once thought. And during the week, in between yoga and meditation and sessions with Natalie, I was able to write a little bit, day by day—even stories that were painful. Words were finding their way onto the page.

I also met Amy Weintraub that week, who was giving a talk about her book *Yoga for Depression*. I was intrigued. Could yoga help with my depression I'd been dealing with for the last two decades?

Some would say the universe was laying out some pretty clear signs to me to open my eyes and pay attention. And so, in typical Rebecca fashion, when the retreat was over, I went all-in on researching and learning more about the science of yoga and meditation—how it could affect my brain, my depression, my life.

I joined a local yoga studio and took as many classes and workshops as I could. I enrolled in a forty-day program that included a yoga and meditation practice five days a week for six weeks. Then I did it a second time. For my 50th birthday, my family gifted me with a longer stay at Kripalu, where I immersed myself in a program to learn yoga philosophy and principles, along with an intensive in Yoga for Depression and Anxiety with Amy Weintraub.

I took me nearly two years, but I was finally able to wean myself off the meds and onto the mat.

The more I practiced yoga, meditation and breathwork, the more memories and stories came to the surface—stories of trauma I'd kept hidden from everyone, including myself. Stories were flowing from my mind through my body to the page. I was creating again. Yoga unleashed me.

My desire to learn more about this connection between yoga and my creative source led me to enroll in a yoga teacher training program. By luck or fate, I had recently landed a job at a yoga studio where Devarshi Stephen Hartman, who had been the dean of Kripalu for over two decades, was offering his exclusive program called Pranotthan Yoga.

Devarshi was the farthest thing from your stereotypical yogi guru in appearance, personality, and teaching style. He in *no way* reminded me of that fake guru I'd fallen prey to in the '70s. I felt safe with Devarshi and his team of teachers, and the Pranotthan yoga training offered a journey of self-awakening unlike any other I had ever gone through in my life.

During the year of training, we spent a lot of time learning about the yogic philosophy of the *Pancha Kosha*. This concept, explained in the ancient Hindu spiritual text called the *Taittiriya Upanishad*, loosely translates to the idea that we experience our world through five energetic sheaths or layers. The outermost layer is our physical body, followed by our subtle energy body. Then our thoughts and emotions come into play, followed by our intuition and inner wisdom, and finally our deep spiritual core. By focusing on and tuning in to each kosha, we learn how to awaken opportunities for self-exploration and creative growth.

It became clear to me that in the past whenever I'd sat down to write, I was connecting with only one layer of experience: my mind. What about the rest of me? What about the stories that were held in my physical body? My energetic body? My intuitive body?

I became fascinated with this concept and began learning as much as I could about the koshas and practices to focus on each one individually and multiple koshas with each other. Movement for my physical body, breath practices for my energetic body, meditations with mudras and mantras for my emotional and intuitive body, and mindfulness practices to awaken my soul.

My writing practice changed. What used to be a 10-minute timed Natalie Goldberg style "write like your life depends on it" (as Natalie would say) had now evolved into a practice of tuning in to my koshas before I sat down to write, and then I wrote like my koshas depended on it!

My writing practice became a healing spiritual practice, and slowly but surely it led me to writing my life stories—including those I had kept under lock and key for decades. With each word, each story that came onto the page, I could feel my body begin to soften, to heal.

This yogic path was inviting me to open up and write my stories. Not just the feel-good happy ones, but all of them—the good, the bad, the beautiful, the ugly. Nothing was off limits.

During my yogic writing practice, I wrote stories about my childhood, the breakup of our family home, my experiences in the cult, my divorce, my struggles with infertility, and my path to parenthood—all of it tumbling out, word after word, story after story. The more I wrote, the more I could feel myself beginning to heal, cell by cell. I was finally able to own my stories and write my memoir.

I now realize the importance of the body and the breath in the writing process. Because words and language are constructs of the mind, most of us associate the writing process only with the intellect, the mind. Language comes from the mind, but the stories are actually stored in our cells. Our body has stored all of our experiences, even those forgotten.

That brings me to this book. I want to share this practice, this path I have found from my mat to my memoir, with anyone who feels blocked in their creative process and is ready to access and write stories that may be stuck in their mind or body. I want you to experience the healing power of yogic writing so that you too can write your life stories and leave your legacy.

CHAPTER 2

WHAT IS A KOSHA?
AND WHAT DOES IT HAVE
TO DO WITH WRITING?

I HAVE TALKED TO YOGIS WHO HAVE BEEN PRACTICING FOR years—decades even—and have never heard the word *kosha* spoken in a yoga class. This is not unusual. In fact, it wasn't until I enrolled in a yoga teacher training program that the pancha kosha philosophy was introduced. And of course it was fun to come up with all sorts of jokes about it. *(Do you have to be Jewish to have koshas? Is there a kosha diet? Do only women have a vijnananmaya kosha?* You get the idea.) But all jokes aside, when my teacher, Devarshi Steven Hartman, explained the pancha kosha theory to our YTT class in a visual and physical way, it made so much sense to me as a human being and a writer.

I thought about how my mind had shut down from writing until I allowed and accepted ALL of me to have space on the page, so to speak. My stories were hidden and would remain silent until my physical body, my energetic body, my emotional body, my witness body, and my inner wisdom were given the opportunity to show up. I am not kidding when I say that memories and old stories began pouring out of me onto the page the more I invited different yogic practices into my writing experience.

So, let's talk about yoga and where the kosha philosophy originated.

Yoga is a set of spiritual practices that is rooted in ancient Indian Hinduism. There are five sacred texts of Hinduism written between 1500 to 900 BC in the language of Sanskrit. One of the sacred texts, called the Upanishads, talks about the relationship between the individual soul (known as Atman) and the universal soul (known as Brahman). The texts say that when we as individual human souls are in alignment with the universal soul, then we are in our truest state of bliss, called Samadhi.

The word *yoga* is derived from the Sanskrit root *"yuj"* meaning *"to yoke or unite."* The primary purpose of yoga as it was originally intended is to unite Atman with Brahman (individual with the universe) in our quest to reach Samadhi—pure bliss and union with the divine. Note that this does not happen simply with a physical practice, as yoga is often thought of today. There are actually eight limbs which are meant to be practiced together to unite Atman with Brahman; the physical postures are only one of the eight, and not the most important one by any regard.

The concept of *"pancha kosha"* is illustrated in the Upanishads to provide a framework for understanding ourselves in this quest for bliss. *Pancha* in Sanskrit means five, and *kosha* means sheath or layer. Simply stated, the koshas are the five layers through which we experience life as human beings from our outermost layer (the physical body we are encased in) to our innermost spiritual core, our soul or *bliss body*. So we, as human beings, are not simply physical bodies walking through life without a purpose. Instead, we experience our world through these five layers in a continual quest to be in union *(in yoga)* with ourselves and the Universe, or God, or Spirit, or whatever you name it.

The koshas are:

1. Annamaya kosha (physical body)

   The first layer of the koshas represents the physical body, including the skin, muscles, connective tissue, fat and bones.

2. Pranamaya kosha (energetic body)

   The second layer represents the energetic or subtle body, also called the *life force body*. This includes the basic, automatic functioning of our bodies—the beating of our heart, the circulation of our blood, and the inhalation and exhalation of our breath.

3. Manomaya kosha (mind body)

   The third layer is our mind, which includes our thoughts, emotions, and the ways we process the world though our senses.

4. Vijnanamaya kosha (wisdom body)

   The fourth layer is our intuition or witness mind. This is where we develop awareness, insight, and consciousness.

5. Anandamaya kosha (bliss body)

   The fifth kosha drops from conscious awareness into the pure bliss body. We've all experienced this at times in our lives—maybe when looking into the eyes of someone we love or getting lost through the process of creative expression in music, art, dance, prayer, or writing.

You may or may not resonate with this ancient philosophy, but I'll bet you know exactly what I'm talking about when I refer to a state of bliss when it comes to creating. We sometimes call this state being "in the flow" or "in the zone." It is when we are in this deep connection with our highest self, when words just flow onto the page almost as if we are being channeled from a source greater than ourselves.

I was at a classical guitar concert recently, and the young man who was playing, Thatcher Harrison, was someone my husband and I have been following since he was eight years old. (He is now twenty-two and studying at the Boston Conservatory of Music.) When he was warming up, I could tell by his facial expression, body language, and the sounds coming out of his instrument, that he was in the zone.

He was totally unaware there were people in the room, and nothing existed except for him and his guitar. He was clearly in alignment with his bliss body, and it showed. At the end of the performance when we went to congratulate him, I told him it felt like he wasn't playing guitar, but rather the guitar *was playing him.*

"Those are the moments I live for," he said.

Being in alignment with our bliss body is when we create at our highest levels, whether we are playing a musical instrument, painting, singing, sculpting, or writing.

A Note about Chakras

The yogic concept of the koshas is sometimes thought to be similar to another line of energy systems in our body called the *chakras. Chakra* is the Sanskrit word for wheel and can be described as energy centers situated along your spine, from the base of your sitting bones to the crown of your head.

While the koshas are thought of as layers of your being, from the outer most physical body to the innermost bliss body, the chakras are wheels of energy that vibrate through all the koshas and have the power of directing the energy throughout the different layers.

Each of the seven chakras correspond to bundles of nerves, major organs, and areas of our body that affect our emotional and physical well-being. If one or more chakra is blocked, then we can feel ill emotionally and/or physically. When all our chakras are open, energy can run through them freely, and harmony exists between the physical body, mind body, and bliss body.

You may have heard the expression "Where awareness goes, energy flows." That pretty much describes the relationship between the koshas and the chakras. Accessing your koshas means being able to focus awareness on these physical and energetic layers. If we are not even aware of our koshas, then we never direct our energy there and the chakras are not awakened.

The seven energy chakras are:

1) The root chakra (*Muladhara* in Sanskrit) is located at the base of the spine and is associated with keeping us grounded, feeling safe and connected with the energy of home and the earth. The color is red, and the vibrational sound is "LAM" (pronounced "lahm").

2) The sacral chakra *(Svadhisthana)* is located a few inches below the belly button and is associated with creativity and sensuality. The color is orange and the vibrational sound is "VAM" (vahm).

3) The solar plexus chakra *(Manipura)* is located below the rib cage and is associated with self-confidence, self-discipline, and igniting your power. This chakra is also responsible for what we call our *gut feeling*. The color is yellow and the vibrational sound is "RAM" (rahm).

4) The heart chakra *(Anahata)* is located in the center of the chest and is associated with love, compassion, and emotional healing. The color is green and the sound is "YAM" (yahm).

5) The throat chakra *(Vishuddha)* is located right above the heart, in the neck and throat area, and is associated with communication and voicing your truth. The color is light blue and the sound is "HAM" (hahm).

6) The third eye chakra *(Ajna)* is located between your eyebrows and is associated with intuition, insight, and clarity of mind. The color is purple or indigo blue and the sound is "OM".

7) The crown chakra *(Sahasrara)* is located on the top of your head and is associated with the connection to the divine or higher power. This chakra is thought to be beyond color and sound, although some say the color is a bright white light. The 'sound' is silence.

In section 2 of this book, I offer practices that not only bring awareness to each kosha, but also work to open the chakras that are particularity associated with writing—the throat chakra which is associated with speaking and writing your truth, and the sacral chakra which enhances creative expression.

CHAPTER 3

How Do You Practice Yogic Writing?

Do you remember how you were taught to write stories in school? First, think about what you want to say. Then outline your thoughts in a linear way, and then write your story according to the plan. I used to write using that linear process, and in fact I got pretty good at it—which is what led me to a path in technical writing. But it wasn't fun (to me), and I was bored out of my mind.

I'm not saying that an outline doesn't help with writing a book—I actually believe book outlines are necessary. But when you sit down to write a first draft, that's not what is going to get you motivated or inspired, or at least that's not what gets *me* motivated and inspired. When we write in this way, we are only accessing one layer of our being, our manomaya kosha (our mind). But here's the kicker—not all our stories reside in our mind!

Today research has shown that our cells hold memories, meaning that stories also reside in our physical bodies. After learning about the koshas, I believe that memories and stories are also held in our energetic and intuitive bodies. This explains the phenomena of people who recall details about events decades after they occurred simply by touching an object, hearing a song, or walking into a room they've never been in before. All of a sudden a vivid memory will come to light about something that happened in that room or one that looked similar. Something similar happens when a person is in a hip opening yoga pose and tears start to well up for no apparent reason as a memory or image comes to the surface. These are all examples of how we hold stories in different layers of our being.

So when we want to write our life stories, both the happy ones and the sad or traumatic ones, our work is to tune into each layer—our body, mind, breath, intuition, and soul—and be open and curious to what comes to the surface.

A yogic writing practice taps into each of the koshas with movement, breathwork, meditation, mudras, mantras, and insightful writing prompts. It is the first thing I do every morning, regardless of where I am or what my daily agenda has in store. It's simple enough to do anywhere, no mat or props required, and it can take anywhere between ten and forty-five minutes. All you need is a journal and pen.

It is important that you do the writing part by hand. Why? Because writing by hand slows you down and makes you more present to the writing process itself. It is also a way to connect the act of writing to the anamaya kosha (your physical body). Not only that, but there have been multiple studies that show that regions of the brain associated with memory are more active when writing by hand as it promotes "deep encoding" in a way typing on an instrument (computer or phone) does not.

Let me repeat that for those who might think they can't write by hand for one reason or another. Unless it is because of a physical incapability (and not just a preference because you're a fast typist or your handwriting is bad), I'm going to insist (well, *suggest* is more like it) that you give it a try. You might be surprised at how much more your brain is willing to open up to memories and creative expression because you are involving your body in the writing process. I like to say, "Stories will travel from the mind *through* the body to the page."

In part 2 of this book, I'll show you several different practices to tap into each of the koshas, so you can pick and choose what works best for your yogic writing practice. You can choose to do a practice that specifically brings awareness to one kosha (like a breath practice, for example), or you can create a practice that brings several different layers together (like movement, then breath, then meditation). It is important to note that bringing awareness to one kosha with a specific practice will simultaneously affect the others.

When we meditate, for example, we might be focusing on our breath which brings awareness to our pranamaya kosha, or perhaps we are directing our attention to a mantra, which brings awareness to our manomaya kosha, our mind body. Both are happening at the same time; we cannot separate one from the other. When we take a walk in nature, we are bringing awareness to our physical body, although it is impossible to walk without breathing or thinking.

Because we are human and each layer is a part of the whole human experience, we cannot separate one from the others. But we can deliberately focus on one kosha to fully allow an experience to unfold before we take pen to paper to see what it might reveal. That is the intention of the yogic writing practice.

My practice generally looks like this: twenty minutes of yoga asana—typically sun salutations, a warrior sequence, and a balancing sequence. This is followed by five to seven minutes of pranayama—usually alternate nostril breathing and a few rounds of kapalabhati breath—followed by five to ten minutes of meditation—sometimes with affirmations or mantras, sometimes silent. Finally, ten minutes of free writing in my dedicated yogic writing journal. I might give myself a prompt, but usually I start with "Good Morning, Monday..." and go from there.

Yoga brings me in touch with my physical body. Pranayama (breath practice) brings awareness to my energetic body. Meditation brings awareness to my mind body and my wisdom body. Then putting pen to paper allows me to blend all that energy together and write from a place of wholeness and truth—my bliss body.

The time varies (sometimes more, sometimes less) but the minimum is a five-minute practice followed by a ten-minute write. More importantly, I allow whatever comes out in my practice to just *be*. With my poses, my breath, my meditation and my words, I surrender wholeheartedly to whatever shows up on my mat—and on the page—without judgment. And what shows up is different every day.

I think of writing in two parts: practice and product. Every morning I do my yogic writing practice, and then I start my day. If something magical comes up in my practice, I will mark it with a sticky post to remind me to come back to it at another time. I might also transcribe something that came up during my practice on to my computer, and then at another time during the day or week, I'll work on crafting it into a story or essay.

Nothing gets in the way of my daily yogic writing practice. It is my time to reunite with my creative soul and to re-member my true self.

Sidenote: I love to practice with music. It inspires me to flow from one pose to the next. My favorite soundtrack for my physical yoga practice includes Krishna Das, James Taylor, K. D. Lang, Girish, and Deva Premal. I also have a spotify playlist called "Yogic Writing With Rebecca" that I invite you to listen to.

soothing effect on the brain and sends a signal that you're safe. When you feel safe, emotions and memories are free to come to the surface.

Here are a few poses I have found to be a powerful way to bring awareness to your anamaya kosha as you begin your yogic writing practice. The names in the parentheses are the Sanskrit names for each pose.

1. Seated Pratapana (six movements of the spine)

Almost every yoga class begins with what is called *pratapana,* which means moving the spine in six ways. Forward bending, backward bending, right side stretch, left side stretch, and right and left twist. If this is the only thing you have time for, it's enough! You can do a pratapana seated on a mat, on a chair, or standing.

Here is an example of a seated pratapana that you can do right from your desk chair.

1. Sit straight up in your chair, with your spine nice and long, and your feet firmly planted on the floor. Tuck your chin slightly, and place your hands on your lap with palms up. Take a long, slow, deep breath in through the nose, feeling your belly inflate. Hold for a second or two, then exhale through the mouth with an audible sound, and feel your shoulders drop away from your ears. Do this three times.
2. Now, on your next long inhale, raise your arms out to the side and overhead and place your palms together. Pause at the top of the breath, and then turn the palms out. On the exhale, lower your arms back down to your side. (Repeat this three times—nice, slow breaths.) Then place your hands back on your lap, palms up.
3. Next, on the inhale: lower your left arm down to the left side and raise your right arm over your head and reach towards the left side for a lateral stretch. On the exhale: Flow right arm back to right side. On the inhale: Lower your right arm to the

CHAPTER 4

TUNING IN TO YOUR KOSHAS

IN THIS CHAPTER, I OFFER PRACTICES TO TUNE IN, OR BRING awareness to, each kosha before you write. In section 2, I describe the practices mentioned here more fully, along with others, so you can try several and see which ones resonate with you.

The Anamaya Kosha (Physical Body)

The first layer of the koshas represents the physical body, which includes your skin, muscles, connective tissue, fat, and bones.

Our body remembers everything. Sounds, smells, touches, and tastes are held in your body, all the way down at the cellular level. Sometimes just a certain movement in an area, like a hip or heart opening pose, might bring up a memory that is stored there and comes flooding back. When we inhabit our bodies in positive ways—such as dancing, yoga, walking, running, or *writing by hand*—we stay in the present moment and open ourselves up to creative inspiration and a positive energy flow. This is why a yogic writing practice ideally includes some kind of physical movement before the pen hits the page. This is especially true if you are feeling stuck or blocked in your writing or when you feel like your creative energy is waning. We've all been there. And the best thing you can do when that happens is—you guessed it—just *move* your body!

Practices that can bring awareness to the anamaya kosha and help you get unstuck or release blocks in your writing include taking a walk, dancing around the room, self-massage, or yoga poses. In section 2 of this book, I offer several different yoga poses or short sequences that can help you bring awareness to your anamaya kosha. If you have a longer period of time to take a yoga class, either online or in person, bring your journal along and take intermittent breaks between poses to write in your journal. I can assure you, stuff will come up!

Yin Yoga

As I shared earlier, my yogic writing practice typically consists of sun salutations, followed by a few balancing poses, and then a warrior sequence. For a deeper (and longer) yoga practice, and one that targets both the anamaya kosha and the manomaya kosha, consider a practice of yin yoga. Yin yoga stretches and targets both the deep connective tissues between the muscles, and the fascia throughout the body. The poses are held for longer periods of time, which allows us to be still and notice what the body and mind are telling us. When we go into a yin pose that opens a part of the body that has been left untouched for a while, such as a hip opener like butterfly or pigeon, deeply stored memories and emotions might resurface. Some yin poses can be challenging in the moment and can lead to a wide array of reactions such as frustration or anger or even sadness accompanied by tears, but afterward it leads to a feeling of complete release.

Acknowledging that it may be difficult and uncomfortable, yet allowing yourself to be with the uncomfortableness is important for the writing process as well. We are not always comfortable writing something that is difficult or painful. We want to stop; we want to move on; we don't want to look there. But with a yin practice we learn that being in a state of allowing uncomfortable feelings to arise,

allowing them to be present, and then feeling the release can be freeing and empowering.

I used to call yin yoga my "are we done yet" practice. Getting into a pose and then feeling all the feels of it, my mind would start to chatter—and loudly—things like *"this sucks, I want out, why am I doing this, I'm done, why does everyone else look like they're enjoying this, I want to go home."* But if I forced myself to stay in the present moment of whatever feelings came up and allowed my body and mind to continue the conversation, the chatter slowly turned into: *"ok, it's getting better, wow—that's a nice stretch, I think I can sink in a little more, this feels kinda good, ahhhhhh, I think I like this."* And the ultimate experience would happen when the class was over and my entire body and mind had gone from uncomfortable to release. That's what I call the *yin afterglow.*

I'll never forget one yin yoga class I went to a few weeks after a beloved aunt had passed away. The very first pose the teacher put us in was the yin version of child's pose, which is done with your knees wide apart, your feet touching, and your forehead to the ground. I got into the pose and within minutes began to cry. I couldn't stop the tears a I started to feel embarrassed when everyone in the class had mo on to the next pose. My teacher, Alicia Barry, whom I adore and later completed her Yin Teacher Training program, came over t rubbed my back, and said "You stay right there."

And so I did.

For the entire hour of the class, I stayed in child's pose cried. When the class was over, I felt the most incredible went home and wrote about my aunt, and I remembered sto her I hadn't thought about for decades. I couldn't stop wr stories were flowing faster than I could write them dow was because I'd been able to be present with my grief and my body to release memories I had been storing.

Wide knee child's pose (*prasarita balasana*) is a v to soothe yourself. Placing your forehead (your 'third just between your eyebrows) on the mat has an inst

CHAPTER 4

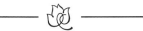

Tuning in to Your Koshas

In this chapter, I offer practices to tune in, or bring awareness to, each kosha before you write. In section 2, I describe the practices mentioned here more fully, along with others, so you can try several and see which ones resonate with you.

The Anamaya Kosha (Physical Body)

The first layer of the koshas represents the physical body, which includes your skin, muscles, connective tissue, fat, and bones.

Our body remembers everything. Sounds, smells, touches, and tastes are held in your body, all the way down at the cellular level. Sometimes just a certain movement in an area, like a hip or heart opening pose, might bring up a memory that is stored there and comes flooding back. When we inhabit our bodies in positive ways—such as dancing, yoga, walking, running, or *writing by hand*—we stay in the present moment and open ourselves up to creative inspiration and a positive energy flow. This is why a yogic writing practice ideally includes some kind of physical movement before the pen hits the page. This is especially true if you are feeling stuck or blocked in your writing or when you feel like your creative energy is waning. We've all been there. And the best thing you can do when that happens is—you guessed it—just *move* your body!

Practices that can bring awareness to the anamaya kosha and help you get unstuck or release blocks in your writing include taking a walk, dancing around the room, self-massage, or yoga poses. In section 2 of this book, I offer several different yoga poses or short sequences that can help you bring awareness to your anamaya kosha. If you have a longer period of time to take a yoga class, either online or in person, bring your journal along and take intermittent breaks between poses to write in your journal. I can assure you, stuff will come up!

Yin Yoga

As I shared earlier, my yogic writing practice typically consists of sun salutations, followed by a few balancing poses, and then a warrior sequence. For a deeper (and longer) yoga practice, and one that targets both the anamaya kosha and the manomaya kosha, consider a practice of yin yoga. Yin yoga stretches and targets both the deep connective tissues between the muscles, and the fascia throughout the body. The poses are held for longer periods of time, which allows us to be still and notice what the body and mind are telling us. When we go into a yin pose that opens a part of the body that has been left untouched for a while, such as a hip opener like butterfly or pigeon, deeply stored memories and emotions might resurface. Some yin poses can be challenging in the moment and can lead to a wide array of reactions such as frustration or anger or even sadness accompanied by tears, but afterward it leads to a feeling of complete release.

Acknowledging that it may be difficult and uncomfortable, yet allowing yourself to be with the uncomfortableness is important for the writing process as well. We are not always comfortable writing something that is difficult or painful. We want to stop; we want to move on; we don't want to look there. But with a yin practice we learn that being in a state of allowing uncomfortable feelings to arise, allowing them to be present, and then feeling the release can be freeing and empowering.

I used to call yin yoga my "are we done yet" practice. Getting into a pose and then feeling all the feels of it, my mind would start to chatter—and loudly—things like *"this sucks, I want out, why am I doing this, I'm done, why does everyone else look like they're enjoying this, I want to go home."* But if I forced myself to stay in the present moment of whatever feelings came up and allowed my body and mind to continue the conversation, the chatter slowly turned into: *"ok, it's getting better, wow—that's a nice stretch, I think I can sink in a little more, this feels kinda good, ahhhhhh, I think I like this."* And the ultimate experience would happen when the class was over and my entire body and mind had gone from uncomfortable to release. That's what I call the *yin afterglow.*

I'll never forget one yin yoga class I went to a few weeks after a beloved aunt had passed away. The very first pose the teacher put us in was the yin version of child's pose, which is done with your knees wide apart, your feet touching, and your forehead to the ground. I got into the pose and within minutes began to cry. I couldn't stop the tears and I started to feel embarrassed when everyone in the class had moved on to the next pose. My teacher, Alicia Barry, whom I adore and years later completed her Yin Teacher Training program, came over to me, rubbed my back, and said "You stay right there."

And so I did.

For the entire hour of the class, I stayed in child's pose and just cried. When the class was over, I felt the most incredible release. I went home and wrote about my aunt, and I remembered stories about her I hadn't thought about for decades. I couldn't stop writing. The stories were flowing faster than I could write them down. I knew it was because I'd been able to be present with my grief and I'd allowed my body to release memories I had been storing.

Wide knee child's pose (*prasarita balasana*) is a wonderful way to soothe yourself. Placing your forehead (your 'third eye' or the spot just between your eyebrows) on the mat has an instant calming and soothing effect on the brain and sends a signal that you're safe. When you feel safe, emotions and memories are free to come to the surface.

Here are a few poses I have found to be a powerful way to bring awareness to your anamaya kosha as you begin your yogic writing practice. The names in the parentheses are the Sanskrit names for each pose.

1. Seated Pratapana (six movements of the spine)

Almost every yoga class begins with what is called *pratapana*, which means moving the spine in six ways. Forward bending, backward bending, right side stretch, left side stretch, and right and left twist. If this is the only thing you have time for, it's enough! You can do a pratapana seated on a mat, on a chair, or standing.

Here is an example of a seated pratapana that you can do right from your desk chair.

1. Sit straight up in your chair, with your spine nice and long, and your feet firmly planted on the floor. Tuck your chin slightly, and place your hands on your lap with palms up. Take a long, slow, deep breath in through the nose, feeling your belly inflate. Hold for a second or two, then exhale through the mouth with an audible sound, and feel your shoulders drop away from your ears. Do this three times.

2. Now, on your next long inhale, raise your arms out to the side and overhead and place your palms together. Pause at the top of the breath, and then turn the palms out. On the exhale, lower your arms back down to your side. (Repeat this three times—nice, slow breaths.) Then place your hands back on your lap, palms up.

3. Next, on the inhale: lower your left arm down to the left side and raise your right arm over your head and reach towards the left side for a lateral stretch. On the exhale: Flow right arm back to right side. On the inhale: Lower your right arm to the

right side and your left arm up over head reaching towards the right side for a lateral stretch on the opposite side. On the exhale: Flow left arm back to left side. (Repeat three times on each side.)

4. Next, on the inhale: Raise both arms overhead (center) and reach towards the sky, then twist to the left, and pause. Exhale: Lower arms and return to center. Inhale: Raise both arms up overhead and twist to the right. Exhale: Lower arms down and return to center. (Repeat three times.)

5. Finally, on the inhale: Slide hands from thighs to knees while rounding your back and bringing chin to chest (cat pose). Exhale: Slide hands back to thighs, raise your chin, open your heart and chest and bring your shoulder blades toward each other, arch your back (cow pose). (Repeat three times, contract and expand.)

6. Now return to the opening pose. Sitting straight up in your chiar, spine erect and long, chin slightly tucked, hands on your lap, palms down, and sit for three normal breaths.

That's it! All six movements of your spine received a nice easy stretch. Now you can stretch your writing muscle! Take out your journal and write, "I am here to..." and see what shows up!

2. Wide-Knee Child's Pose *(Prasarita Balasana)*

This pose is wide-knee child's pose with extended arms. It is truly a pose to surrender. To come into this pose, kneel onto the floor, and spread your knees as wide apart as is comfortable for you. Keep your big toes touching one another. Lean forward at the waist and place your forehead on the floor. If your hips pop up, don't worry about it. As you stay in the pose, keep inviting your hips to meet your heels. *(If you have any knee issues, place a block or cushion under the sitting bones to lift the buttocks away from the heels. A bolster under the torso can also help.)*

Your arms can take several positions: straight over your head or by your side with palms up and moving toward your feet and relaxing your shoulders toward the ground. You can also rest your hands on top of one another and have your forehead rest on your hands rather than the mat.

The key concept of doing this pose in the yin style is to allow your body to melt into the pose. There is no forcing, striving, or pushing in yin yoga—just being present to where you are in the moment. The key is to sink into the pose so that your body and your mind will *let go*. Surrender and be present to what comes to the surface.

When you're ready to come out of the pose, take out your journal and write, "I am willing to…"

3. Pigeon Pose (or Sleeping Swan) *(Eka Pada Rajakapotasana)*

Trauma, tension, stress, old emotions, and vulnerabilities are often stored in our hips. When we feel deep emotions like sadness, fear, or anger, our unconscious reaction is to clench our jaw or fists, and our hips are alerted to take a fight-or-flight response. We might even bend forward and raise our knees to protect our core. (Have you ever noticed that when a child is sad or scared, they curl up and cry? Adults do the same, though it may not be as dramatic or obvious.)

When our hip muscles have been clenched tightly over a long period of time (*you may not even be aware of how long you've been doing this*), they shorten and never fully release the tension. By stretching the hip muscles, it allows not only a release in the physical body, but also the trapped emotions that have been stored there as well. That is why if you write immediately after a hip opening pose that has released stored emotions, you might be surprised at what shows up on the page.

To come into the pose, begin on all fours and then bring your front foot close to the inner groin area, and slide the other leg behind you. If you have space under your hip, use a blanket or other soft prop to support you. Press your hands into the mat and rock back and forth to bring your weight into your hips. If the front knee is sensitive, flex your front foot to relieve pressure. You might also lean forward and rest your head on your mat, a blanket or a block. Inhale and exhale slowly through the nose. Try to stay in this pose for at least five breaths.

To come out of the posture tuck your back toes under, inhale and pull your front leg back. Rest in child's pose after the posture as a gentle counter pose. Repeat the same steps on the opposite side.

If this pose is too uncomfortable, you can get the same effect by laying on your back, knees raised, and bringing your legs into a figure-4 position.

When you're ready to come out of the pose on both sides, take out your journal and write, "I feel..." and see what comes up!

4. Warrior II Pose (*Virabhadrasana II*)

There are three main warrior poses in yoga (warrior I, II, and III). They each have a completely different feel and bring about different energies. Warrior II, in my humble opinion, is one that is incredibly empowering and makes me feel like *I can do anything* when I'm in the pose. It is a full body pose that targets nearly all your muscles and strengthens your legs, glutes, hips, core, chest, shoulders and arms. Holding the pose for an extended period of time also helps develop endurance—and that is something we writers need!

It's an interesting pose to practice before you write. Tune in to your inner warrior, and then channel that feeling of strength and power onto the page.

To begin, stand with legs wide apart (more than shoulder width) and your feet facing forward. Turn your right foot out about 90 degrees, so that your toes are pointing away from your body. Turn your left foot in slightly to help you keep stability and balance. Keeping your balance, raise your arms out to the sides, with your palms facing the ground. Look toward your right hand. Focus on the tips of your fingers as you stretch out your arms and extend out through your hands.

Now bend your right knee. Your thigh should aim to be parallel to the floor, and your knee should be above the ankle. Press into your feet, and let your hips sink down toward the floor.

Hold the pose and *feel your power.* Then straighten your legs. Practice the pose on the opposite side by repeating the steps, but turn your left foot out to 90 degrees, bend your left knee, and look toward your left hand.

Now that you have embodied this warrior energy, take out your journal and answer this prompt: "I know..."

The Pranamaya Kosha (Energetic Body)

According to the pancha kosha philosophy, the second layer represents the energetic or subtle body, also called the *life force*. The subtle body is what keeps the physical body alive. It includes the beating of your heart, the circulation of your blood, and of course breathing!

The word *prana* in Sanskrit means breath or life force, and *ayama* means to control. Therefore, *pranayama* can be defined as practices to control the breath. Now obviously you don't have to think about breathing; if you are alive, you're already doing it. However, by bringing awareness to your breath, you can stimulate your parasympathetic nervous system which controls your body's ability to relax (as opposed to the sympathetic nervous system, which controls the body's fight-or-flight response).

There are several breathing practices to both stimulate or quiet the mind, which is why pranayama (breath practice) can be so powerful before you sit down to write. If you're feeling anxious, a breathing practice can calm you down. If you're feeling tired, a different breath practice can energize you. Breath practices can also increase memory, improve circulation, and promote oxygenation of the blood—all good things for a writer!

It's quite remarkable what manipulating your breath patterns can do. Here are a few of my favorites that I often include in my yogic writing practice.

1. Box (or Square) Breath

This breathing practice is probably the simplest one you can learn, and it's quite effective to calm you down and reduce anxiety. The box breath is a nice practice right before meditation, or you can use this breath *as* your meditation practice. This practice can also help you quiet your mind before going to sleep. If you do a few rounds of box breathing before you write, you might find your handwriting is slower and more deliberate, and your mind isn't jumping around which allows you to capture your thoughts in a calmer way.

Here's what you do:

> Take a seat anywhere you're comfortable—on a chair, on your bed, or on a cushion. Place one hand on your heart and one hand on your belly. Relax your shoulders, wiggle your jaw, and take a deep breath in through your nose and exhale through your mouth with an audible exhale to release all tension. Lower your gaze or close your eyes.

> Now take a long slow breath in through your nose, feeling your belly expand with a count of 1–2–3–4. Hold for a count of 1–2–3–4 and then slowly exhale through your nose for a count of 1–2–3–4 and hold again for the count of 1–2–3–4.

> Repeat. Inhale for 4, hold for 4, exhale for 4, hold for 4.

> It might help to imagine drawing a square starting from the bottom left corner. On the inhale, draw a line up the left side of the square; on the hold draw a line across the top of the square; on the exhale draw a line down the right side of the square; then on the hold bring your hand back to the bottom left corner, as if you are drawing a box.

2. Alternate Nostril Breathing (*Nadi Shodhana*)

In Sanskrit, *nadi* means energy channel, and *shodhana* means cleansing. Therefore, *nadi shodhana* is also referred to as *channel cleansing breath*. We cleanse our energy channels in order to restore *balance* in the left and right hemisphere of our brain.

The right nostril activates the sympathetic branch of the autonomic nervous system, which is our fight-or-flight response. The left nostril tissue stimulates the parasympathetic nervous system, the one associated with rest and relaxation. With alternate nostril breathing, we balance both parts of our nervous system, as well as our masculine and feminine energy, yin and yang, circular and linear, and so forth.

When your energy channels are out of balance you feel anxious, frustrated, or just *off*. When you are in a state of balance and calmness, your mind is able to retrieve memories that may have been hidden or difficult to access.

To practice alternate nostril breathing:

1. Start by placing your thumb gently on your right nostril and take a deep inhale through your left nostril.

2. Then with your ring finger close off your left nostril (so both nostrils are closed) and hold your breath for a few counts, then release your thumb from the right nostril and exhale through your right. Pause.

3. Now inhale through your right nostril, place your thumb back on the right nostril (so both are closed) then release your ring finger from the left nostril and exhale through the left. Pause.

4. Continue this practice for a minimum of ten rounds. Inhale/hold/switch/exhale. Repeat.

Feel the breath (prana) cleansing both nostril channels and slowing your heart rate down. After ten rounds of alternate nostril breathing (or when you feel ready), pick up your pen and journal and see what surfaces.

I like to move from alternate nostril breathing to a prompt that also works with balancing, or opposites, such as: "*I remember, I don't remember,*" or "*I feel, I don't feel,*" or "*I need, I don't need.*"

3. Skull-Shining Breath (*Kapalabhatti*)

This breath practice is used to awaken energy and focus. *Kapala* in

Sanskrit translates to *skull* and *bhati* means light. So when you are practicing this exercise, think of a bright light entering your skull to wake you up! This is a great practice to use when you're writing and feel depleted or if you feel like you're drifting away from the point of your story. Doing a few rounds of kapalabhatti breath can be rejuvenating and bring you back into focus. It's a great caffeine replacement!

Do not practice kapalabhati if you are pregnant or if you have high blood pressure, acid gastric issues, heart disease, abdominal pain, or if it makes you feel dizzy. It's always best to start slowly, and then with time you can increase the speed and number of rounds.

To practice kapalabhati breath:

Sit comfortably in an upright position and place your hands on your lower belly. If you're sitting in a chair, make sure to have both feet on the ground. Start by first noticing your regular inhale and exhale. Stay with that for a few breaths. Then think about lifting the crown of your head toward the heavens, feeling a lift to your body and the back of your spine.

1. Take a deep, cleansing breath in through your nose and out through your mouth.
2. Now inhale again through your nose, filling your belly with air about halfway full.
3. Forcefully expel all the air from your lungs through your nose in short spurts while drawing your navel in toward your spine. Don't worry about the inhalation; it will happen naturally. Take ten to twenty forceful exhale breaths like this to complete one round.
4. After completing the round, relax with your eyes closed and observe the sensations in your body. Then allow your breathing to return to normal, and if you choose you can begin another round. The count and rounds can be increased gradually over time, but don't do more than three rounds of ten as a beginner.

4. Bees Breath (*Bhramari*)

This breathing technique gets its name from the black Indian bee called *bhramari*, as the exhale will sound like a swarm of bees. This breath practice works wonders if you're having problems concentrating. It's one of my go-to's when I want to write but my brain is insisting on doing cartwheels instead. You create a buzzing sound during this practice, which works to calm your nervous system almost instantly. This is a wonderful practice to interrupt the negative thought spirals that sometimes accompany writers. It will give your inner critic a shove goodbye. Who wants to be in a swarm of bees? You might also find this breath practice to be very calming, depending on whether you do it with a high-pitched hum or a low-pitched hum.

You can also add a mudra (hand gesture) known as the *shanmukhi* or womb mudra to bring a deeper introspective quality to the practice, which taps into your wisdom body (*vijnanamaya kosha*) as well.

To practice bees breath:

1. Place your index fingers on your ears. There is cartilage between your cheek and ear. Place your index fingers on the cartilage.
2. Close your eyes and take a deep inhale. As you exhale, gently press the cartilage while making a humming sound like a bee. You can make either a low-pitched or a high-pitched sound. Try them both and see which one works better for you. I tend to use the high-pitched hum during the day to bring me into focus and concentrate and the low-pitched hum at night to relax.

To use the hand mudra:

Bring your index fingers to the brow points. Place your middle fingers gently over the eyelids. Place your ring fingers at the edge of the nostrils (not pressing the nostrils), pinky fingers at the edge of the lips, and thumbs press the outer cartilage near the cheekbone into the ear canals. Once your hands are in place, practice the inhale and exhale with either the high or low pitch to activate this powerful bees breath.

The Manomaya Kosha (Mind Body) and Vijnanamaya Kosha (Wisdom Body)

I group these two koshas together because they both have to do with the mind. The manomaya kosha is the lower mind, or the reactive mind. The vijnanamaya kosha is the higher mind, or the reflective mind. The manomaya kosha is our thoughts and emotions and internal chatter, and our vijnanamaya kosha is our inner wisdom and intuition that doesn't get caught up in the chatter. Rather, it acts as a witness to the experience.

Paying attention to both our reactive mind (thoughts and emotions) and our reflective mind (intuition and wisdom) when writing a story is a key component to connecting with your reader. We write our story to share our unique thoughts, emotions, and experiences, but the magic happens when we find a way to connect our experience with a universal one. We do that by adding a reflective piece to the thoughts and emotions that arise from our stories. Tuning into our manomaya kosha and our vijnanamaya kosha before we sit down to write can help us with this process.

We bring awareness to both our manomaya kosha and our vjnanamay kosha through meditation, mantras, mudras, chanting, and proprioceptive writing. In part 2 of this book, I will introduce several of those practices in the Twenty-One Day journey. I mention a few here that are simple and effective to target both koshas in one practice.

1. Meditate with a Mantra

I'm sure you've heard by now the value of a meditation practice. "Just 10 minutes a day" is what I was told would be the key to reaping the benefits of a meditation practice. *"Just"* ten minutes, I thought. Have you tried to sit and not think about anything for ten, or even five minutes? Not so easy, is it?

Our brains have a job to do, and that is bring ideas to the surface. I've been told that we have somewhere around two thousand thoughts per hour. Per hour! So just to run some numbers here, if you sit down to meditate for ten minutes, which would be approximately two hundred thoughts you will need to *quiet*! Ha! That's probably not going to happen, right?

Meditation is not about *not* thinking—that's impossible. The goal of meditation is really to find little snippets of stillness between the thoughts. And you actually realize you are having them when you come out of them! It's pretty cool when you come back to the present moment and realize —*Hey, I was somewhere else for this past two minutes, three minutes, five minutes.* The more you meditate, the more quickly you will come to these places of stillness.

One of the best ways to get to these places of stillness is to give your mind something to think about, or bring awareness to. Whether that is counting your breath (as in the box breathing method explained above) or using a mantra to give your mind something to focus on. This is a key component to transcendental meditation. A mantra is a word or phrase you repeat during meditation. You can speak, chant, whisper the mantra, or simply think about it in your mind.

To practice a meditation with a mantra:

Take a moment to feel your sitting bones on your chair or cushion. Take a couple of deep, cleansing breaths, and relax your shoulders. Begin to slowly inhale and exhale through your nose. Close your eyes, and then repeat these words to yourself as you breathe:

On the inhale: *I am here.*

On the exhale: *Here I am.*

You can also choose one word or sound to begin your meditation practice. After a while, you might let that sound go and just come into silence. It doesn't have to mean anything, it can simply be a sound, such as "Om" or any other word or phrase you choose. You could also use the sounds associated with the seven chakras or energy centers in your body to repeat in a meditation practice. That would be: lam, vam, ram, yam, ham, om. (Note: the *a* in *lam* and the other seed syllables is pronounced with an "ah" sound.)

As you sit in meditation with a silent mantra, you might find yourself drifting off to sleep, *or* you might find thoughts coming to mind. Then you might be telling those thoughts to go away! The conversation your mind can have with itself when you are trying to meditate is actually kind of funny. That conversation is a clear example of how the manomaya kosha and the vijnanamaya kosha are in conversation with each other. The reactive mind holds the thoughts and emotions, and the reflective mind bears witness to them. They are like sibling rivalry in a way, although not with a negative connotation. Your mind might go to the thought of what you want to do when you're finished meditating, and then your witness body will respond with— *Oh, that's interesting; you're thinking about what you want to do next.*

The truth is that thoughts coming in are also a part of meditating, and instead of getting upset or frustrated that it is happening, just simply notice it and bring yourself back to the mantra or counting. The more you practice meditation, the more you will be able to find moments of stillness. Be patient with yourself and start small. Despite what I was told about a ten-minute minimum, I am here to say that even a minute or two of a meditation practice can be beneficial.

You can find several different types of meditations on apps or YouTube that are free. Meditating with mantras or affirmations is a positive way to tune into both your manomaya kosha and your vijnanamays kosha, your reactive and your reflective mind.

2. Metta Meditation (Loving-Kindness)

Metta meditation is a type of Buddhist meditation, also known as loving-kindness meditation. It is about bringing unconditional love to people in your life without any expectations of receiving anything in return. If you have a meditation app on your phone, or YouTube, you can find several loving-kindness meditations to guide you. One of my favorite teachers is Sharon Salzberg. She is a pioneer in the field and has played a crucial role in bringing metta meditation into mainstream culture since the early 1970s.

You can also practice it on your own without a guide.

1. Find a comfortable seat, and breathe naturally, slowly and evenly. Begin by bringing loving-kindness to yourself by quietly or silently saying the following phrase:

    "May I be safe. May I be healthy. May I be happy. May I live with ease".

2. Now think about someone you love. Think about this person (or animal) and repeat the phrase with the intention of sending loving-kindness to that soul.

   "May you be safe. May you be healthy. May you be happy. May you live with ease."

3. Next bring your attention to someone neutral in your life, someone you might see daily or weekly but don't have much of a relationship with. It might be someone who works at your neighborhood store or bank, maybe your postal carrier, maybe your child's teacher. Repeat the same phrase with the intention of sending loving-kindness to this person.

   "May you be safe. May you be healthy. May you be happy. May you live with ease."

4. Now bring your attention to someone with whom you don't necessarily get along with—someone with whom you have conflict. Repeat the same phrase with the intention of sending loving-kindness to this difficult person. (Note: If this step is too painful, then go back to bringing loving-kindness to yourself.)

   "May you be safe. May you be healthy. May you be happy. May you live with ease."

5. And finally, repeat the same loving-kindness mantra to all human beings and animals on this planet.

   "May all beings be safe. May all beings be healthy. May all beings be happy. May all beings live with ease."

I find this to be a beautiful meditation practice that can change your mood and energy from negative to positive. A metta meditation practice can bring awareness to the vastness of the world around you and leave you with a feeling of hope. And who doesn't need more of that in the world today?

3. Proprioceptive Writing

Proprioception is our body's ability to sense itself or know where it is in space. Proprioceptive writing, a practice based on the book *Writing the Mind Alive* by Linda Trichter Metcalf, takes this one step further and explores the mind by "writing what you hear and listening to what you write." Whatever shows up in your mind's eye, you record as is. And when something appears that might be vague or perhaps hold a hidden meaning, you break it open by asking what is called the *proprioceptive question*.

I am not going to go in detail about all the components of proprioceptive writing. You can buy the book or take a class on it. There are distinct components, rules, and rituals to the practice, such as the type of paper you write on and the type of music that must play in the background.

I don't subscribe to all the rules of PW, but the one that I do use often in my writing practice is what is called *asking the proprioceptive question*, which is "What do I mean by ...?" You do this at intervals in your writing when something comes up that brings you to a pause. Asking the question brings a special awareness to what you meant by a particular word or phrase. You actually write the words: "What do I mean by ...?" followed by the word or phrase in question.

This prompts you to take a deeper dive and become more aware of what you are exploring through your writing, and it can bring your story into a direction you didn't expect. In part 2 of this book, I will include this practice so that you can experiment with it. Propreoceptive Writing is one that brings acute awareness to your vijnanamaya kosha (your inner wisdom).

The Anandamaya Kosha (Bliss body)

Wouldn't it be awesome if I could give you one specific practice that would allow you to get *in the zone* at will? Believe me, if there was a simple way to do it, we'd be there all the time! But of course, we are all unique human beings, and each one of us has a unique way of getting in touch with our own bliss body. You know when you're tapping into it; you can feel it!

When we are in union with our bliss body, we feel a connection to a power greater than ourselves. When all of our koshas are in alignment, we are whole and perfect. When we write from our bliss body, words just fall onto the page as if we are being channeled by a greater power. That is the bliss we aspire to.

I can tell you this: when you practice yogic writing in a consistent manner, you will get into the zone more often and more easily. That has been my experience and that of many of my students as well. Writing is like a yoga practice. You get on the mat; you greet the blank page. You meet your resistance, and then you let it go.

The more you let it go, the more you'll find yourself in the flow.

Putting it all together: *Take your koshas for a walk in nature!*

Recently I had the opportunity to spend some time at Kripalu, a retreat center nestled in the Berkshire Mountains. I had been thinking and writing about this pancha kosha philosophy, so I thought I'd take a walk with the intention of bringing awareness to all my koshas and see what I might experience.

Here is what happened: First, the simple act of walking ignites your physical body, your anamaya kosha. Your muscles, your bones, your heart, and all the other organs of your physical body come for the ride when you are walking. I notice my breath as I walk uphill and recognize the changes in my breath pattern, my pranamaya kosha. My physical body and my subtle body are in alignment as I walk slowly, one foot forward on an inhale, the other foot forward with the exhale—a slow, mindful, walking meditation.

This of course brings awareness to my manomaya kosha, my mind body, and I begin to count my steps. And then I think, *Why am I counting steps?* I answer my own question and remind myself that I've always liked to count steps or anything, really. I've always been a counter! *When did this start?* I wonder. *Was it because my father used to tell me that I'm good at math so I should become a math teacher?*

See what happened there? My manomaya kosha, my mind, started to do what our minds do. It begins to chatter; it reacts to what is going on. Then my reflective mind, my inner wisdom and witness, kicks in with a story, and begins to dissect and reflect what is happening. All of this happens simultaneously of course, but I am aware of it and fascinated at what is happening.

I then head down the hill and notice something I've never seen before in all the times I've been to Kripalu. There is a small garden with four statues, which I assumed were there to represent the four teachings of Buddhism. My mind begins to tell the story of these statues, and I am thinking about why they are here and why is it that I've never seen them before. *Why now? Why do I need to see these statues now?* I reflect further and say to myself that this feels like I am discovering things about myself every year, the smallest little things, and the biggest things too. The view of the mountains is so expansive, and the smallest pinecones on the ground in front of these four statues are so simple.

I then notice a tree that has grown wild and resembles a cave, so I crouch down and go inside. Clearly I'm not the only one who has discovered this cave tree because there are candles, little statues, and scraps of cloth with beautiful sayings written on them. This is a shrine, it seems. As I take it all in, my physical sheath is uncomfortable. Because I am crouching, my breath pattern changes and I feel slightly claustrophobic. My mind starts to play like a movie, and I'm overcome with a feeling of being unsafe. I am slightly panicked.

Then my inner wisdom kicks in and says, *You are safe here today. Why do you feel unsafe? What does this remind you of?*

I think that it sort of reminds me of a womb, which should do the opposite of make me feel unsafe. It should make me feel comfortable, right? Then I begin judging myself. My vijnanamaya kosha begins to witness what I am doing, and my manomaya kosha judges how I feel—it's not the right way to feel.

My physical body and my breath body are both on the same page, and I decide to crawl out of the tree cave. I feel relief once I'm out, and my breath changes. I look at the view once again and feel small in this huge garden of nature. I like that feeling. It feels safe.

I pay attention to each layer as I listen deeply and reflect on each story, I then begin to write. I write about all of this, and I notice how fast my hand is moving and that my breath is still unsteady. I decide to do a breath practice that will calm me, so I begin the practice of alternate nostril breathing. It calms me right down, slows my heart rate, and makes me feel centered and balanced—back to my true self, not the self that was afraid or panicked or getting wrapped up in a story, but rather the self that is aware of the beauty around me and the beauty within.

I walk a little further down the path and come across a tree I had never seen before. I see a plaque that describes what kind of tree it is. It is called the grandmother tree, and I immediately feel a kinship with this tree. I have 4 grandsons and 1 granddaughter. I adore my grandchildren, and my times with them are some of the happiest moments of my present-day life.

I also get sad when I think of them because I don't live very close to them so can't see them as often as I would like. Both feelings come waving across me now as I gaze at this grandmother tree. There are stories here. There are letters to write to my granddaughter and my grandsons. There are letters to write to my children too. I want them to each know me and my unconditional love for them. I know I need to write these letters now. The pull is great. This was a simple one: the tree was called the grandmother tree, so it immediately brought me to the place of wanting to write to my children and grandchildren.

Sometimes the cues are so obvious, and sometimes we need to dig a bit more to find the stories we need to write. We need to walk in nature, being open to what is there, curious about what is in front of us and what it brings to mind, and open to what shows up, without judgment. Or we at least need to notice when judgment shows up and then let it go.

So what about the fifth kosha, the bliss body? As I walk in this beautiful spot of nature, do I have moments of bliss? You bet your kosha I do! Some moments I just sit on a chair or a rock and just stare, breathe, and feel the vast beauty of what is around me. I feel gratitude, and gratitude is the one thing that can bring you to your bliss knees every time.

I begin to write again. I write about being unattached to the outcome of my experience. I don't want my nature walk to end. I didn't want my walking meditation to end. I don't want my time at Kripalu to end. I wanted to pick up a stone from the meditation path and put it in my pocket, just to remember this moment. But my practice here is to appreciate the moment as it is, and that is good enough. Or rather, that it is perfect—just as it is.

When you allow yourself to be present and pay attention to your koshas individually and together, you feel whole. You can feel what your body is doing, what your breath is doing, what your mind is doing, and what your intuition is telling you—your entire experience all together. Similar to a traditional Russian stacking doll; the outer layer opens to one inside, and then that one opens to another one, and then another, until you reach the smallest doll at the center that doesn't have a seam. You cannot open it. It is whole and perfect as it is.

As I am.

As you are.

SECTION 2

Twenty-One Day Writing Journey

INTRODUCTION TO THE TWENTY-ONE DAY JOURNEY

Now that you have a better understanding of what yogic writing is all about, let's put it into practice!

In this next section, I have included twenty-one different yogic practices and writing prompts to inspire you to write your life stories. You can do them in any order, although please start with Day 1. You can do them at any time during the day when you can carve out fifteen quiet minutes for yourself.

This Twenty-One Day program is based on the age-old belief that it takes twenty-one days to fully form a new habit. However, there is also ample research that says a new habit takes a little more than two months with as many as 254 days until it's fully formed. So while I can't guarantee that after twenty-one days of daily writing you will have formed a habit, I can tell you this: If you enjoy it, you will continue. If you see that it's working, you will continue it. If you miss a day, not a big deal. If you miss a week, not a big deal. You can pick this up at any time and jump back in. You can write every day or every other day or once a week.

The bottom line is that you write! And every day that you write is a day you will feel good about your progress, regardless of what you wrote. The craft of writing is like a muscle. You have to use it over and over again in order for it to get better and stronger.

And before you know it, you will have written a collection of life stories that you feel proud of. You will have a jumpstart to your memoir.

Julia Cameron says that writing is like the weather. "Just as a good rain clears the air, a good writing day clears the psyche. There is something very right about simply letting yourself write. And the way to do that is to begin, to begin where you are."

So let's begin!

First, a couple of rules:

- Each day will begin with a delicious five-minute yogic practice that taps into one or more of your koshas. It might be a meditation, a breath practice, or a simple yoga pose, followed by a writing prompt. *Even if the yogic practice is unfamiliar to you, I suggest you give it a try before you move on to the prompt.* Think of it like extra chips in a chocolate chip cookie. The cookie will be good either way, but why not go for the extra yum?

- After the five-minute practice, set your timer for ten minutes, and *write by hand.* Why? Because writing by hand slows you down and makes you more present to the writing process itself. It's also a way to connect the act of writing to the body. And when your body is involved in the process, you get to the flow state with greater ease.

- Write for ten minutes without taking your pen off the page— even if that means writing the prompt over and over again, or even writing "I can't write today" or whatever else that comes out. It's *fine.* You are still writing. And the more you train yourself to write for ten minutes daily, the more your brain will eventually give in and let it go. It will, trust me. Trust yourself.

- If the prompt takes you down a road and a detour is in front of you (meaning you start to write something that has nothing to do with the prompt) by all means *take the detour!* There is a reason why your inner wisdom directed you to explore something different, so trust in that and enjoy the journey.

- Once your timer goes off, *if you want to keep going* because something happened and you are being guided or channeled by something greater than yourself, *well then, keep going!* You're *in the zone* (your anandamaya kosha—your bliss body!) and that's where we *all* want to be! Enjoy it!

- When you're finished, if something interesting showed up, you can transcribe your writing from your journal into a document on your computer. If you want to play a bit and edit, rearrange, add or delete sentences, feel free—that's the fun part! However, the main purpose here is to cultivate a *practice* of writing, not writing a perfect essay. Some of these prompts will engage you to keep going and write a story, and some of them will simply be to flex your writing muscle. Remember that however you show up on the mat and on the page is exactly how it should be.

Swami Kripalu says, "The highest spiritual practice is self-observation without judgment."
Write your stories. Write them from the heart. And do so without judgment.

PS If you're a Facebook user, you can join my free Facebook group, Yogic Writing with Rebecca. There is a community of yogic writers there that share thoughts about writing as well as actual stories they have written using this process. It's a fun place to hang out!

DAY 1

I AM A WRITER

I am not in charge of whether or not my work is great,
or how people will like it. I am only in charge of the
process. I came here to be a writer, and so I write.
—Elizabeth Gilbert

THE FIRST THING I ASK OF MY STUDENTS WHEN WE BEGIN A
workshop or writing group together is to say these words out loud:
"My name is _____, and I am a writer."

Sometimes someone will giggle a little bit, or someone's cheeks
will turn the slightest shade of pink, or I notice someone rolling their
eyes and smiling, as if to say, "Well, not really." Or they might even say,
"I want to be a writer, but I haven't published anything."

To which I always respond, "If you love to bake, you are a baker;
you don't have to own a bakery. If you love to run, you are a runner;
you don't have run a marathon. If you write, then you are a writer.
Being a writer has nothing to do with whether you have published a
book."

There are words and stories inside of you—both fact and fiction—
and your job is to give them the space and opportunity to be birthed
onto the page. Whether or not someone else reads them is secondary.

Say it with me, "My name is _____ and I am a writer!"

Step 1: Breathe

(Pranamaya kosha)

You may be feeling just a bit of anxiety now that you are about to embark on a new journey to begin writing your life stories. For that reason, this first practice is all about calming down and breathing into the fact (yes, *fact*) that you are a writer.

In this first practice, we will tune in to your energetic body, your pranamaya kosha, with a simple breath practice called box breath. By bringing awareness to your breath, you stimulate your parasympathetic nervous system, which controls your body's ability to relax. Once you are relaxed, you can put pen to page in a calming, less anxious way.

To begin, set a timer for five minutes.

Take a seat anywhere you're comfortable—on a chair, on your bed, or on a cushion. Place one hand on your heart and one hand on your belly.

Relax your shoulders, wiggle your jaw, and take a deep breath in through your nose. Then exhale through your mouth with an audible exhale to release all tension.

Do this two or three times, just to settle in. Close your eyes if that feels OK.

Now take a long, slow breath in through your nose, feeling your belly expand with a count of 1–2–3–4, hold for a count of 1–2–3–4, and then slowly exhale through your nose for a count of 1–2–3–4, and hold again for the count of 1–2–3–4.

Repeat. Inhale for 4, hold for 4, exhale for 4, hold for 4.

If you are a visual learner, it might help to imagine drawing a square starting from the bottom left corner. On the inhale, draw a line up the left side of the square; on the hold, draw a line across the top of the square; on the exhale, draw a line down the right side of the square; then on the hold, bring your hand back to the bottom left corner.

When your timer goes off, grab your journal and pen, and go on to step 2!

Step 2: Write

Pick up your pen and open your journal, and *smile!* (I'm not kidding—it really does help!) Then set your timer for ten minutes and write the following phrase at least five times.

I am a writer. I am a writer. I am a writer.

Now write this prompt:

I want to write about ...

Keep your hand moving! Don't take the pen off the page for the entire ten minutes! Remember, if nothing comes up, just keep writing the prompt: *I want to write about ... I want to write about ... I want to write about ...*

Step 3: Transcribe and Share

When your timer goes off (or when you're finished writing), *if* you choose, you can transcribe whatever you wrote into a document on your computer and begin to play with it. Maybe you want to expand on something that came out, or maybe you want to just let it sit and marinate as it is. The important part of this first practice is that you began your writing journey. So thank yourself for showing up!

Tomorrow you can move on to practice 2.

PS You can also join and share your writing in the private Facebook group Yogic Writing with Rebecca.

DAY 2

I REMEMBER

> A writer gets to live twice. First we live, and
> then we write about how we have lived. Often
> the second time is the real life for a writer. It
> is then we get to claim our existence.
> —Natalie Goldberg

EVERY MEMOIRIST I HAVE STUDIED WITH, INCLUDING NATALIE Goldberg, Julia Cameron, Dani Shapiro and Nancy Aronie all use this one simple prompt to jog memory and bring a story to life: *I remember.*

Life stories begin with a memory, whether it is an event that occurred yesterday or twenty years ago. Interesting fact: It is impossible for the average human brain to record with total accuracy something that happened just minutes ago. The brain edits memories relentlessly, updating the past with new information, so our memories are constantly changing and being rewritten.

The *good* news is that what we remember most are the feelings and emotions about the event. The *better* news is that feelings and emotions are universal. So even if our reader has never experienced an event similar to what we are writing about, they will connect with the feeling behind it.

The *best* news is that the more you write about a particular memory, the more you can retrieve the details about it, and it can lead to more memories that have been hiding within. So writing can actually *improve* memory. How about that?

For example, when I hear the song, *Baby I Love Your Way*, I'm transported to the front seat of my 16-year-old boyfriend's Ford Pinto cruising down the road with the windows rolled all the way down. The details become clear as day, right down to the clothes I am wearing, the feeling of my hair blowing across my face, the smell of the cigarette butts in the ashtray, and my boyfriend's raspy voice singing along with Peter Frampton. That one scene jogs my memory into multiple stories of those long-gone days, and the more I write the more I remember.

Step 1: Breathe

(Pranamaya Kosha)

We will begin our practice today by tuning in to our pranamaya kosha with a breath practice called Nadi Shodhana, or alternate-nostril breathing.

In yogic breathing practices, we pay attention to which nostril we are inhaling from because of the effects it can have on our nervous systems and which hemisphere of our brain is stimulated. Both ancient yogi science and modern science agree that there is a relationship between the left side of the body and the right hemisphere of the brain, as well as the right side of the body with the left hemisphere of our brain.

The primary function of alternate-nostril breathing is to restore *balance* in the left and right hemispheres of your brain and your sympathetic and parasympathetic nervous system. When you are in a state of balance and calmness, your mind is able to retrieve memories that may have been hidden or difficult to access.

To read more about Nadi Shodhana breath practice, refer to the Pranamaya Kosha section in part 1.

1. Start by placing your thumb gently on your right nostril, and take a deep inhale through your left nostril.

2. Then, with your ring finger, close off your left nostril (so both nostrils are closed), and hold your breath for a few counts. Then release your thumb from the right nostril, and exhale through your right. Pause.

3. Now inhale through your right nostril, place your thumb back on the right nostril (so both are closed), then release your ring finger from the left nostril and exhale through the left. Pause.

4. Continue this practice for a minimum of ten rounds. Inhale/ hold/switch/exhale. Repeat.

Feel the breath (prana) cleansing both nostril channels and slowing your heart rate down. After ten rounds of this alternate nostril breathing (or when you feel ready), pick up your pen and journal, and *smile!*

Step 2: Write

Set your timer for ten minutes. Now write the prompt: *"I remember ..."*

Keep your hand moving and pen on the page—don't worry about spelling or grammar; just keep writing *"I remember ... I remember ... I remember ..."* repeatedly until something surfaces. Your brain will eventually kick into gear, and something will emerge. It may be a random list of anything and everything you happen to remember, or one memory in particular might lead you down a path that compels you to write more about it. Either way, just go with the flow. *I remember. I remember.*

When you feel like you've come to a natural pause, return to the alternate-nostril breath practice for ten more rounds.

Inhale left/hold/switch/exhale right.

Inhale right/hold/switch/exhale left.

Then go back to the page and write the prompt, *"I don't remember ..."*
Keep your hand moving and the pen on the page, and keep writing, *I don't remember ... I don't remember ... I don't remember ...* until something surfaces.

Step 3: Transcribe and Share

When your timer goes off (or when you're finished writing) if you choose, you can transcribe whatever you wrote into a document on your computer and begin to play with it. Maybe you want to expand on something that came out, or maybe you want to just let it sit and marinate just as it is. You can always come back to this raw writing on another day.

Remember that you can also join and share your writing in the private Facebook group Yogic Writing with Rebecca.

DAY 3

HOPE

You can trap bees on the bottom of Mason jars without
lids because they don't look up, so they just walk around
bitterly bumping into the glass walls.
Go outside. Look up.

—Anne Lamott

HAVE THERE BEEN TIMES IN YOUR LIFE WHEN YOU MIGHT HAVE
felt stuck at the bottom of a Mason jar, bitterly bumping into walls,
feeling like there was no way out? I know I have. Times during my
teen years when I was carrying secrets that should never have been
mine to keep. Or when I was dealing with infertility and feeling like
there was no path to my becoming a mother. Or during the dark days
of the covid pandemic when I couldn't visit my grandchildren or my
mother for months on end, wondering how and when we would ever
get back to "normal."

I remember my husband and I would go outside in the middle of
the night just to look up at the stars in the sky, knowing that everyone
on the planet, regardless of who they were and where they lived, were all
under the same sky. We all saw the same sun. We all saw the same moon.

Hopelessness often stems from being or feeling alone. Realizing
that we were all in it together gave me hope for humanity. Hope for
a new beginning, a new path, a new life. Sometimes all it takes is to
look up.

Step 1: Meditate

(Manomaya and Vijnanamaya kosha)

In this meditation, we are going to use the mantra associated with the concept of "Be here now" (thank you, Ram Dass) to keep you in the present moment and find snippets of stillness. This meditation allows you to witness your body and mind, which brings awareness to your manomaya kosha and your vijnanamaya kosha.

Take a moment to feel your sitting bones on your chair, take a couple of deep cleansing breaths, and relax your shoulders. Set your timer for five minutes, and slowly inhale and exhale through your nose. Repeat these words to yourself as you breathe.

On the inhale: "I am here."

On the exhale: "Here I am."

Each time you inhale feel the crown of your head rising slightly towards the heavens and on the exhale feel your body grounding into your seat. Continue to recite the mantra "I am here. Here I am."

If (OK, *when*) your mind begins to wander, bring it back by repeating the phrases on both the inhale and the exhale.

Step 2: Write

Think about a time in your life when you might have been stuck in a situation and had difficulty finding a way out. Like the bees on the bottom of the Mason jar, was there a time when you felt like there was nowhere to go? What did it take for you to look up from your life? What gives you hope in the world today?

Set your time for ten minutes and write the following prompt.

"What gives me hope today is..." or *"I felt hopeless when…"*

Step 3: Transcribe and Share

When your timer goes off, if you choose, you can transcribe whatever you wrote into a document on your computer and begin to play with it. Maybe you want to expand on something that came out, or maybe you want to just let it sit and marinate just as it is. You can always come back to this raw writing on another day.

Remember that you can also join and share your writing in the private Facebook group Yogic Writing with Rebecca.

DAY 4

———— ✿ ————

LOVE

Love and compassion are necessities, not luxuries.
Without them, humanity cannot survive.
—Dalai Lama

HAVE YOU EVER BEEN IN A ROOM FULL OF PEOPLE YOU DIDN'T KNOW and yet felt a strong loving presence in the air? I felt it when James Taylor sang the words, "Shower the people you love with love," as the Dalai Lama came onto the stage one afternoon in a Boston hotel venue. I was alone, but at that moment I suddenly felt deeply and lovingly connected to every person in that room. We all swayed and sang along. I've also felt it during a group meditation practice, a peaceful protest, and even at a World Series baseball game. (Go Red Sox!) There is no denying the power of love is strong—and contagious (in a good way).

Remember when the pandemic shut down cities all over the world and people were singing and applauding hospital workers from their balconies? Buildings lit up, and signs of encouragement were plastered across the nation. Amidst the divide in our country, *love* was (and is!) still in the air, and even with masks on our faces, we can breathe it in.

Step 1: Meditate with a Mantra

(Manomaya kosha)

Today's yogic practice will tap into the manomaya kosha (the mind). A simple way to do that is by using a mantra in your meditation. The mantra works as an object of focus. It is a toy to keep the monkey-mind busy and allow it to become more calm and centered.

You can choose any one word or phrase as your mantra—something that resonates with you. You can even use a line from a poem or song. I sometimes use the mantra, "Shower the people you love" on the inhale, "with love" on the exhale. (Thank you, James Taylor).

Another mantra that is sweet to use to anchor your mind in meditation:

Inhale: "I breathe in love."

Exhale: "I breathe out fear."

After five minutes, or whenever you feel ready, set your timer for ten minutes, pick up your pen and journal, and *smile*!

Step 2: Write

Do you remember an experience in your life when you felt a collective love in the air? Or perhaps a time someone showed compassion and kindness to you when you least expected it? If nothing comes to mind, just think about *love*. List all the things you love in your life (people, places, animals, experiences), past or present, and when you get to one where you feel like your heart is opening up, go in deeper.

Set your timer for ten minutes, and write down these words: "I love ..."

Remember, just keep writing the prompt, "*I love ... I love ...I love ...*" until you land somewhere that begs you to dive in.

Keep your hand moving!

Don't take the pen off the page for the entire ten minutes.

Step 3: Transcribe and Share

When your timer goes off, if you choose, you can transcribe whatever you wrote into a document on your computer and begin to play with it. Maybe you want to expand on something that came out, or maybe you want to just let it sit and marinate just as it is. You can always come back to this raw writing on another day.

Remember that you can also join and share your writing in the private Facebook group Yogic Writing with Rebecca.

DAY 5

LETTING GO

In order to be a good writer, you have to be willing
to be a bad writer. You have to be willing to let it all
out, every little detail that catches your fancy ... The
creative process is a process of surrender, not control.
—Julia Cameron

SO YOU'VE GOT THE HANG OF THIS NOW, RIGHT?

Find your spot.

Find your center.

Find your pen and journal, and *go*!

Fifteen minutes fly by! Or ... maybe not? Remember that much
like a yoga practice, every day you show up will be different. Don't
expect too much. Be patient, and just let whatever happens happen.
Be willing to be a bad writer. Be willing to write the worst stuff that
ever hit the page. Be willing to write *"a shitty first draft,"* a phrase
popularized by Anne Lamott.

This is a *practice*. And as with any practice, the goal is not
perfection—it is simply to keep moving forward, one thought, one
detail, one word at a time. And to let go of any preconceived ideas of
what your writing should look like. Surrender to whatever shoes up,
and accept it as is.

60

Step 1: Yoga (Child's Pose)

(Anamaya kosha)

Today's practice is bringing awareness to the anamaya kosha, the physical body. To tap into the physical body, we practice simple yoga poses or sequences.

Today's pose is wide-knee child's pose with extended arms. It is truly a pose of surrender. If it's not comfortable for you to stay in this pose for an extended period of time, try placing a blanket or towel under your thighs or rest your forehead on a blanket or cushion. If you have any knee issues, a modification for this pose is to place a block or cushion under the sitting bones to lift the buttocks away from the heels. A bolster under the torso can help too.

The key here is to sink into the pose so that your body and your mind will *let go.*

Surrender.

Option: You can stay in the pose for two to three minutes, and then slowly travel your tented fingers to your right side, sinking into a side body stretch. Stay there for a minute or so, then back to the middle, and then the left side, then back to the middle.

Relax. Sink in. Let go.

Step 2: Write

Set your timer for ten minutes, and write down the following words.

"I am ready to let go of…" or *"I surrender to…"*

If nothing comes to mind, just keep writing the prompt, *I am ready to let go of … I am ready to let go of … I am ready to let go of …*

Keep your hand moving!

Don't take the pen off the page for ten minutes.

Step 3: Transcribe and Share

When your timer goes off (or when you feel like your writing has come to a close) you can choose to transcribe whatever you wrote into a document on your computer. This idea of letting go of something in your life may have brought up a memory or an idea that you can expand upon and craft into a life story.

Remember that you can also join and share your writing in the private Facebook group Yogic Writing with Rebecca.

DAY 6

BLISS

> Nothing is more important than reconnecting with
> your bliss. Nothing is as rich. Nothing is more real.
> —Deepak Chopra

OR, AS I LIKE TO SAY, "BLISS HAPPENS!"

You know the bliss I'm talking about, right? It's when you are writing from a place that you can't quite explain, when words just fall out of you and onto the page and you are merely a scribe, channeling something greater than you.

Have you ever experienced a feeling like that—a connection between you and a power greater than you? Perhaps it happened through writing or maybe drawing, dancing, playing a musical instrument, praying, or meditating.

I believe that writing is a spiritual practice. And just like any other spiritual practice, it can be a bridge from the self to the universe. We connect to ourselves by bringing thoughts and words from our mind, through our body, and onto the page. And we connect with others through sharing those words; through sharing our stories. We find our bliss, and we become the conduit to others finding theirs.

So let's do it. Let's connect—and make bliss happen.

Step 1: Silent Meditatation

(Vijnanamaya kosha)

This silent meditation taps into your vijnanamaya kosha, your wisdom body. This relates to our ability to observe our lives from a somewhat objective point of view, without judgment. When we do this, we can more easily connect with others, forgive others, and be able to witness what we are doing and how we are continually evolving into better versions of who we are in this lifetime.

(Set your timer for five minutes—or longer if you wish.)

1. Find a comfortable place to lie down for this meditation in what is called a *savasana* pose (corpse pose). Take a couple of deep, cleansing breaths, inhaling through your nose and exhaling through your mouth. Clench your fists, your arms, your shoulders, and your face. Hold for a few seconds, and then let it all go with a deep exhale to release any tension you are holding. Do that a couple more times.

2. Wiggle your jaw to release any tension there. Then start to inhale and exhale naturally, through your nose. Take a slight pause at the top of the inhale and the bottom of the exhale.

3. Continue to breathe naturally, bringing your awareness to your body from your toes, to your feet, your calves, your thighs, your belly, your hands, your arms, your shoulders, your neck, your face, your forehead—all the way to the crown of you head. As you settle your awareness on each part of your body, energetically release any tension you might find. Continue to breathe naturally for the remainder of the five minutes.

Step 2: Write

Think about one or two blissful moments you have experienced in your life. It doesn't have to be anything huge; it can simply be a moment when you felt deeply connected to yourself, your higher power, or the universe.

Write about any one of them.

"A blissful moment was…" or *"I feel bliss when…"*

Step 3: Transcribe and Share

When your timer goes off, if you choose, you can transcribe whatever you wrote into a document on your computer and begin to play with it. Maybe you want to expand on something that came out, or maybe you want to just let it sit and marinate just as it is. You can always come back to this raw writing on another day.

Remember that you can also join and share your writing in the private Facebook group Yogic Writing with Rebecca.

DAY 7

WARRIOR

If you have the courage to start, you
have the courage to succeed.
—Mel Robbins

ARE YOU FAMILIAR WITH THE CLASSIC 1980s FILM *PRIVATE
Benjamin*? There is a scene where Goldie Hawn has a meltdown about
all the things she's missing from her old life, and she says, "I wanna put
sandals on! I wanna go out to lunch!"

Haven't we all been there at one time or another, especially
during the pandemic we lived through these past few years? I know
I have! Remember when going out to lunch wasn't even an option?
Restaurants were closed, meetups canceled, no hugging allowed.

There are so many things that have changed since the onset of
the pandemic, but right now I try to find joy in things that are new to
this way of life and learn a lesson or two about what I may have taken
for granted. I'm not a spoiled princess who suddenly finds herself
scrubbing toilets in the army—not by a long shot. But just as Judy
Benjamin emerges into a new warrior version of herself, so shall we.

We are all warriors. At one point or another in our lives, we
have all been warriors. We are still all warriors. Life is a battlefield
in many ways, but the way we choose to "battle" can be through
courage and love.

Step 1: Yoga (Warrior II)

(Anamaya kosha)

Today's practice is bringing awareness back to the anamaya kosha; the physical body. This pose is called Warrior II, and let me tell you—there's no way you don't *feel* like a warrior when you are in it! It's an interesting pose to practice before you write. Tune in to your inner warrior, and then channel that feeling of strength and power onto the page.

1. To begin, stand with legs wide apart (more than shoulder width) and your feet facing forward. Turn your right foot out about 90 degrees, so that your toes are pointing away from your body. Turn your left foot in slightly to help you keep stability and balance. Keeping your balance, raise your arms out to the sides with your palms facing the ground. Try to ensure that your arms are in line with your shoulders.

2. Look toward your right hand. Focus on the tips of your fingers as you stretch out your arms and extend out through your hands. Now bend your right knee. Your thigh should aim to be parallel to the floor, and your knee should be above the ankle. Press into your feet, and let your hips sink down toward the floor.

3. As you inhale, rotate your palms toward the sky, and straighten your right leg. As you exhale, rotate your palms back down to face the floor, bend your knee, and sink your hips toward the ground.

Do this with the flow of your breath four or five times. Inhale, straight leg, palms up. Exhale, bend knee, and sink hips, palm faced down. Go slowly.

Then hold the pose for a few seconds and *feel your power*. Then straighten your legs. Practice the pose on the opposite side by repeating the steps, but turn your left foot out to 90 degrees, bend your left knee, and look toward your left hand.

When you feel ready, set your timer for ten minutes, pick up your pen, and journal. And *smile*!

Step 2: Write

Think about times in your life when you have been a warrior. Perhaps you didn't know it at the time, but on reflection you can see that *yes* you were a *warrior*! And no doubt you came through even stronger than before.

Write about one of those times. Or write about the warrior you are *today*.

Set your timer for ten minutes, and write down the following words.

"*I am a warrior...*" or "*I was a warrior when ...*"

Keep your hand moving! Don't take the pen off the page for the entire ten minutes.

Remember, just keep writing the prompt: *I am a warrior ... I am a warrior ... I am a warrior ...* and see what comes out!

Step 3: Transcribe and Share

When your timer goes off, you can transcribe what you wrote into a document on your computer and begin to play with it. Maybe you want to expand upon something that came up. This idea of being a warrior can make for a juicy life story!

Remember that you can also join and share your writing in the private Facebook group Yogic Writing with Rebecca.

DAY 8

MENTORS

So long as anyone remembers me, or my
teaching, I shall be among the living.
—Gregory Parkos

GREGORY PARKOS, MY UNCLE, WAS MY FIRST TRUE MENTOR.
Although he has been gone for over a decade, I still hear his voice
guiding me to this day. Sometimes I feel his gentle push when I'm
trying to finish a project (he was a very goal-driven person), and
sometimes I hear his comforting words when I find myself in a
conundrum of one kind or another.

My uncle and I shared a love of reading and writing. He always
kept a running list of books he planned to read before he died—and
even assigned each one a month in which he would read it. When
someone recommended a new book to him he'd say, "I may not have
time to get to that one, but I'll put it on the list."

When I read *Tuesdays with Morrie* by Mitch Albom, it reminded
me so much of my uncle that I sent him a copy, along with a note that
said, "Put this one on the list." He called me a week later to tell me
he'd bumped it to the top of his list since I'd sent it to him, and he was
so glad he had. We had long conversations afterward about Morrie.

Uncle Greg believed in a daily writing practice. Every morning at
the crack of dawn, he sat at his desk and wrote for thirty minutes. It
might have been a story, a memory, or just something he was thinking

about. (Does this sound familiar?) He always carried a little black book and pen in his pocket, and he would whip it out to jot down any note, thought, or phrase that seemed important.

"For my book," he would say.

He did what he promised he would—wrote and self-published a book titled *I Was Thinking: Vignettes of a Life Well Spent*. His intention was to write 365 stories, one for every day of the year, and publish the stories as a trilogy with each book containing four months of stories. The first book was January 1 to April 30. There are stories about not only his life, but some about my grandparents, my mother, my aunts and uncles, and my cousins—family members I never knew, stories that would have been lost forever. This book means the world to me, as it has connected me to my family of the past and present.

At a family party in July 2009, Uncle Greg brought a big box of his newly published book and gave an autographed copy to everyone in the family. I never saw him prouder than he was on that day. Uncle Greg died unexpectedly two months later, but the legacy he left is one my family and I treasure.

A mentorship is a special relationship, and although I've had several writers and teachers I look up to and learn from, no one could ever take the place of my dear Uncle Greg.

He will always remain among the living to me.

Step 1: Metta Meditation (Loving-Kindness)

(Manomaya kosha)

If you have a meditation app on your phone or YouTube, you can find several loving-kindness meditations you can use to guide you. One of my favorite teachers is Sharon Salzberg. She is a pioneer in the field and has played a crucial role in bringing metta meditation into mainstream culture since the early 1970s.

Here is a link to one of her 15-minute metta meditations:

https://insighttimer.com/sharonsalzberg/guided-meditations/lovingkindness-meditation

Or read through the following script first, and then try it yourself.

1. Find a comfortable seat, and breathe naturally, slowly, and evenly. Begin by bringing loving-kindness to yourself, and silently repeat the following phrase one or two times. "May I be safe. May I be healthy. May I be happy. May I Live with ease."

2. Now bring your attention to someone you love. Someone that brings a smile to your face. It could be a person in your life, or one that has passed or one you've never met that inspires you. Repeat the phrase with the intention of sending loving-kindness to that person. "May *you* be safe. May *you* be healthy. May *you* be happy. May *you* live with ease."

3. Next bring your attention to someone with whom you have conflict. Someone that is difficult for you to have a relationship with. Or someone you know that is having a difficult time in their life right now. Repeat the same phrase, with the intention of sending loving kindness to this person. "May *you* be safe. May *you* be healthy. May *you* be happy. May *you* live with ease."

4. Bring your attention to someone neutral in your life, someone you might see daily or weekly but don't have much of a relationship with. Maybe someone at a store you frequent,

or a teacher, or a neighbor. Repeat the same phrase with the intention of sending loving-kindness to this person. "May you be safe. May you be healthy. May you be happy. May you live with ease."

5. And finally, repeat the same loving-kindness mantra to all human beings and animals on this planet. "May all beings be safe. May all beings be healthy. May all beings be happy. May all beings live with ease."

Step 2: Write

Think about a mentor in your life—perhaps a parent, grandparent, or other family member who was there for you when you needed advice or a helping hand or love. Maybe a teacher or someone you worked for or even a famous person you've never met could be a mentor.

If no one comes to mind, maybe *you* are a mentor to someone in your life. Write about that relationship.

Set your timer for ten minutes, and write.

"Someone who has made a difference in my life…" or *"I am making a difference in the life of…"*

Keep your hand moving! Don't take the pen off the page for the entire ten minutes.

Step 3: Transcribe and Share

When you're finished writing, you can choose to transcribe whatever you wrote into a document on your computer and begin to play with it. Maybe you want to expand on something that came out, or maybe you want to just let it sit and marinate just as it is. You can always come back to this raw writing on another day.

Remember that you can also join and share your writing in the private Facebook group Yogic Writing with Rebecca.

DAY 9

FEAR

Fear and courage are like lightning and thunder;
they both start out at the same time, but the fear
travels faster and arrives sooner. If we just wait a
moment, the requisite courage will be along shortly.
—Ralph Keyes

LET'S TALK ABOUT THE F-WORD.

F–false

E–expectations

A–appearing

R–real

Haven't we all come face to face with the emotion of fear once or twice in our lives (ha!)? And if we are not aware that we are afraid, it may manifest as anxiety.

Someone once told me that anxiety is emotions you haven't identified or allowed yourself to feel. Anytime I feel myself becoming anxious about the future I take a moment to be with myself and identify what I am feeling. I write down all my feelings and all my fears, regardless of how irrational they might be. I look at the list. I see what things on the list I have no control over and which ones I can do something about.

Let me give you a (silly) example. At the start of the Covid-19 pandemic, when we first started to hear about the toilet paper shortage, I panicked. *Oh no, we won't have toilet paper!* I wrote that on my "fear list." Then I looked through our supply closet and saw that we had twelve rolls of toilet paper. We had three people living in our house. If we each used one roll of toilet paper every week (which is way overestimating) then we were good for an entire month! Is it rational that in one month there still won't be toilet paper available? No!

Writing down my fears (and believe me, toilet paper wasn't the only one) allowed me to look at each one individually and think about where it came from, whether it was rational, and if there was anything I could actually do about it.

Writing about our fears with curiosity and interest can help us discover why we hold onto them. It can also bring up some deep-rooted stories from our childhood or life experiences, where any one particular fear may be rooted. By writing about my fear of the toilet paper shortage, I recalled early days when my parents first divorced, and my father left without giving my mother any financial support. We lost our home and my mother had to find a job for the first time in her life. She left notes on the fridge for my sisters and I like, "Don't eat all the yogurt in one day!" We've laughed about this years later, but now I recognize it as a deep-rooted fear that we wouldn't have enough food for the week.

Writing a fear down not only acknowledges that you have it, but it takes the fear from the dark places in the back of your mind where it has power over you and brings it outside of you, where *you* have power over the fear. Writing about your fears releases them from your mind to the page, and you may find that most of your fears really are just *false expectations appearing real.*

Step 1: Breathe and Smile

(Pranamaya kosha)

Come into stillness. Find a posture that is relaxed and at the same time alert. Feel your body touching the surface beneath you and your feet touching the floor. Scan your body and see if you can relax and soften any areas of tension.

Let your awareness come to your breath; feel your chest and belly expand and contract with the in breath and the out breath. No need to control the breath or change it; just experience it as it is.

Now take a nice, slow inhale, feeling the nourishing aspects of oxygen in your body. As you breathe in, smile. Try to make your smile follow the path of your inhale.

Hold the breath at the top for a few seconds, and as you do imagine the smile radiating throughout your body.

Then slowly exhale, releasing all the tension you have in your body. Feel your shoulders drop, your jaw soften, and release the smile.

Do this again!

Repeat this breath, smiling on the inhale, pausing to feel the nourishment through your body, and releasing all tension on the exhale. If you feel any tension in a particular area of your body, when you inhale, imagine the oxygen going right to that specific area and dissolving the fear you might be holding there. When you exhale, imagine releasing that fear from the spot where you felt it, all the way down to your toes.

Pay attention to how much better your body feels each time you do this exercise. Once you've hit all the specific tension points, focus on the entire body again. Feel the breath and the smile bringing you peace, healing, and nourishment. Feel the exhale releasing all the tension in your body.

When you're ready, pick up your pen and journal, and—you guessed it—*smile*!

Step 2: Write

Set your timer for ten minutes, and write, "I am afraid that …" Try to write at least five sentences.

The idea isn't to write down everything you're afraid of. Instead, reflect upon *one* of your identified fears that you're ready to let go of now.

Think about and write responses to the following questions.

What is my earliest memory of this fear?

Was it triggered by an event in my life?

In what ways—negative and positive—has having that fear affected my life?

Step 3: Transcribe and Share

When you're finished writing, if you choose, you can transcribe whatever you wrote into a document on your computer and begin to play with it.

Remember that you can also join and share your writing in the private Facebook group Yogic Writing with Rebecca.

DAY 10

DREAMS

They say dreams are the windows of the
soul. Take a peek and you can see the
inner workings, the nuts and bolts.
—Henry Bromell

HAVE YOU EVER HAD REALLY VIVID DREAMS? OR A DREAM THAT
was so frightening it woke you up out of a deep sleep? What about a
dream within a dream?

Fascinating, aren't they?

We dream because it is good for us. Dreams help our brains make
sense of our waking lives. The best time to try to recall your dreams
is in the first ninety seconds after you wake up, before the memory
goes away. Dream experts recommend trying to keep your body in the
exact same position you were in when you woke up, as this will help
boost your dream memory.

After two minutes spent replaying and piecing together the
thoughts, feelings, and images from your dream, write them down
right away—or perhaps record them on your phone. Either way,
keeping a dream journal is a fun thing to experiment with!

What are you dreaming about these days—either when you are
sleeping or awake? Do you remember your dreams?

What have your dreams revealed to you?

Step 1: Breathe

(Pranamaya kosha)

Remember when you were told to count sheep to fall asleep? The reason it worked was not because of the sheep, but because you were counting your breaths, and that actually works! So if you're having trouble falling asleep, try counting your exhales, starting with ten and counting backward until you reach one. When you get to one, if you're still wide awake, do it again. You might even start at twenty and count each exhale all the way down to one.

You could also try this breath practice magic. This is called bee's breath *(bhramari)*, and it works wonders—not just to help you fall asleep, but also to help with anxiety and concentration. It's one of my go-tos when I want to write but my brain is insisting on doing cartwheels instead. You create a buzzing sound during this exercise, which works to calm your nervous system almost instantly.

1. Place your index fingers on your ears. There is a cartilage between your cheek and ear. Place your index fingers on the cartilage.
2. Close your eyes and take a deep inhale. As you exhale, gently press the cartilage while making a humming sound like a bee. You can make either a low-pitched or a high-pitched sound. Try them both and see which one works better for you. (I prefer the high pitch when I use this during the day, but at night I use a low-pitched hum to help me fall asleep.)
3. Continue the same pattern six or seven times—or more!

Step 2: Write

Set your timer for ten minutes and write the following phrases.

"I am dreaming about..." or *"My dreams have revealed..."*

Keep your hand moving! Don't take the pen off the page for the entire ten minutes.

Step 3: Transcribe and Share

When your timer goes off, you can transcribe what you wrote into a document on your computer and begin to play with it. Maybe you want to expand on something that came out, or maybe you want to just let it sit just as it is.

Remember that you can also join and share your writing in the private Facebook group Yogic Writing with Rebecca.

DAY 11

TRADITIONS

Without our traditions, our lives would
be as shaky as a fiddler on the roof!
—Joseph Stein

THE IMPORTANCE OF TRADITION IS BEAUTIFULLY CAPTURED BY
the opening lines of the film *Fiddler on the Roof*. Despite this
affirmation of tradition, the movie centers on the cultural assimilation
that threatened to put an end to the Jewish identity.

I think of this often in my own Greek family, as I witness with
every generation our traditions being watered down. I am guilty of
this with my own children. I was raised by Greek parents and part of
the Greek Orthodox Church. However, when my parents got divorced
and my world changed in so many ways, going to church was no longer
part of my life. I drifted away from the religion and the traditions that
went along with it and never really went back. My husband is from
Uruguay and brought up in the Jewish faith, so our family traditions
are not rooted in any one religion or culture. Instead, we pick and
choose the ones we like from both, and we make up our own, too!

Think about your family traditions. How has your identity been
shaped by the traditions your family kept when you were a child and
those you have carried on (or not) in your own family?

Step 1: Meditate

(Manomaya kosha and Vjnanamaya kosha)

This meditation practice comes from the teachings of spiritual leader and poet Thich Nhat Hanh.

Take a seat anywhere you're comfortable—on a chair, on your bed, or on the floor. Place your hands on your lap, palms up, and close your eyes. Gently breathe in through your nose, exhale through your mouth and sigh. Relax your shoulders. Wiggle your jaw. Do this a couple more times—inhale through your nose; exhale with a sigh.

Now take a nice, long, deep breath in through your nose, expanding your belly as you inhale, and say to yourself, *I know I am breathing in.* Hold the breath at the top for a second or two, and then slowly exhale through the nose, saying to yourself, *I know I am breathing out.* Hold for a second or two when you have fully exhaled.

Then repeat—nice and slow and even.

I know I am breathing in.

I know I am breathing out.

Practice this for ten rounds or five minutes.

When you're ready, pick up your pen and journal, and *smile!*

Step 2: Write

Set your timer for ten minutes, and write one of the following prompts.

"A tradition I love is..." or *"I remember celebrating..."*

Step 3: Transcribe and Share

When your timer goes off (or when you're finished writing) if you choose, you can transcribe whatever you wrote into a document on your computer and begin to play with it. Maybe you want to expand on something that came out, or maybe you want to just let it sit and marinate just as it is. You can always come back to this raw writing on another day.

Remember that you can also join and share your writing in the private Facebook group Yogic Writing with Rebecca.

DAY 12

PIVOTAL MOMENTS

The pivotal moments in your life are always made up of
smaller pieces, things that seemed insignificant at the
time, but in fact brought you to where you needed to be.
— Elizabeth Norris

LET'S THINK ABOUT PIVOTAL MOMENTS IN YOUR LIFE. SOME MIGHT
be obvious, like the day you were married or divorced, the birth of a
child, a significant move, and so on. Those are easy to list. They have
clear dates. The before and after lines are cut and dry.

But then there are other more subtle pivoting moments of clarity
that shifted your perspective, made you take a detour, or changed
you in some way that you might not have even realized until years
later. Those are the pivoting moments that define who you are. Those
pivoting moments are your stories.

I'll share an example of a moment in my life when I couldn't see
the path in front of me, and then after a pivot, a path was revealed.

It was New Year's Eve, 1995. My husband and I were at a party
with friends in South America, but instead of counting down the New
Year with excitement and joy, we were alone outside on the balcony,
and I was sobbing. After years of fertility treatments trying to get
pregnant, it just wasn't happening. I was convinced I would never hold
a baby in my arms again.

My husband held me in his arms and said, "Do we want to be pregnant, or do we want to have a baby?"

That question, that moment, was the pivot to our path to creating our family through adoption. At that moment, my entire perspective shifted. Our adoption journey began that day, and a year and a half year later, I was cradling a baby in my arms.

My perspective changed, which opened a path for me to see beyond where I was stuck. That one conversation was a pivotal point in my life that led me to be a different person.

This, by the way, is what writing a memoir is all about. A memoir is not an autobiography, not a story of your entire life, but rather a story of a pivotal moment (or moments) in your life when you started out as person A, and something happens that changes you to become person B. I am oversimplifying, but the point is every single person could write multiple memoirs! In fact, we can *all* write one about the pivotal moment in our lives living through a pandemic. Many of us are still pivoting. It is clearly something that has changed us all.

Step 1: Breathe

(Pranamaya kosha)

Today we are going back to the basics—a very simple, yet powerful, breath practice called diaphragmatic breathing. This practice helps increase the supply of blood and nutrients to your muscles, blood, and bones. It relieves tension in your body and slows down your heart rate, which in turn helps release stress and anxiety. It's great before a writing practice because it helps clear your mind, open your heart, and settle your being.

1. Sit in a comfortable position or lie on the floor. Relax your shoulders.
2. Put one hand on your chest and the other on your belly.

3. Breathe in slowly through your nose for about three or four counts, feeling the air move through your nostrils into your abdomen, making your belly expand. Think about your belly moving outward while your chest remains relatively still.

4. Purse your lips (as if you're about to drink through a straw), press gently on your stomach, and exhale slowly.

That's it! Repeat these steps for about ten rounds or five minutes. When you're ready, pick up your pen and journal, and—*smile!*

Step 2: Write

Today I invite you to write about a pivotal moment in your life, when something happened that changed you from person A to person B.

If you feel stuck, start by making a list of five pivotal moments that come to mind. Then pick one—either one that is happening now or any other one on your list.

Set your timer for ten minutes and write down the following words. *"A pivotal moment in my life was when ..."*

Keep your hand moving! Don't take the pen off the page for the entire ten minutes.

Step 3: Transcribe and Share

When your timer goes off (or when you're finished writing) if you choose, you can transcribe whatever you wrote into a document on your computer and begin to play with it. Maybe you want to expand on something that came out, or maybe you want to just let it sit and marinate just as it is. You can always come back to this raw writing on another day.

Remember that you can also join and share your writing in the private Facebook group Yogic Writing with Rebecca.

DAY 13

FIRST LOVE

> I am glad it cannot happen twice, the fever
> of first love. For it is a fever, and a burden,
> too, whatever the poets may say.
> — Daphne duMaurier

AHHH... FIRST LOVE.

No matter how fragile your memory might be, there's a pretty good chance that you remember the first time you fell in love. Or at least the first time you *thought* you were in love.

Psychologists believe that most people experience a 'memory bump' somewhere between the ages of thirteen and twenty-six. This memory bump happens at a time when we are experiencing all kinds of firsts such as first kiss, having sex, driving a car, etc. These memories tend to be more impactful because they occurred when our memory was at its peak.

We learn so much from our first love and bring that knowledge into every relationship thereafter. How it feels to be wanted and desired; how we want (or don't want) to be treated by someone else; and (perhaps) how to get through a broken heart.

My first love happened when "the new guy from California" arrived at my high school. His wild, frizzy hair smelled like Herbal Essence shampoo. His skin was flawless, not a blemish in sight. He had full lips and perfectly straight teeth. He wasn't wearing a t-shirt or a football jersey like the other boys. Instead, he wore a silky, Hawaiian dress shirt like he was on vacation, with light blue (tight) corduroy pants. A thin leather choker with a silver IXOYE pendant hung around his neck. No other boy in school wore a choker. And he was barefoot! Walking in school barefoot.

That was it.

I instantly fell in love.

For my 15th birthday, he gave me a wooden dollhouse that he made in shop class, saying it was a replica of the house we would live in someday, happily ever after.

The love was fierce, as were the breakups. Again and again.

The years eventually moved us both in different directions and we lost touch with one other. Many years later I moved back to my hometown, and the week before my daughter would start the very same high school where Wade and I met, an old friend texted me: "Do you remember Wade?" she asked. "I'm on my way to his funeral." My heart sank.

You never forget your first love.

May he rest in peace, barefoot and carefree.

Steps 1: Yoga

(Anamaya kosha)

I've said it before, and I'll say it again: Our bodies remember everything. Our stories reside within us and are stored at a cellular level. Someitmes all it takes to open up and write is to simply move your body! You can do this by going for a walk or run, dancing around the room, or practicing some simple yoga stretches.

Try this yoga writing practice to warm up your spine, your shoulders, your hips, and stimulate your throat chakra. You can do this entire practice on your chair.

Round 1

- Sit with your feet firmly on the ground, back straight, hands on thighs. Inhale deeply, raising your right arm. With an exhale, reach your right arm toward the left side, and extend your left arm toward the floor, feeling the stretch in the right lateral side of your body.

- Inhale and rise to center, and exhale and lower the arm.
- Then inhale and reach your left arm to the center, and on the exhale, lean to the right side extending the right hand toward the floor. Practice this three times on each side.
- Now place your right hand on left knee, inhale rise up from core, exhale twist gently to the left; core first then shoulders, neck and head last. Stay in the twist for one inhale/exhale count. Then back to center. Place left hand on right knee and inhale; exhale and gently twist to the right. Twist three times on each side.
- Seated Cat/Cow. Inhale and round back and bring chin to chest, sliding your hands toward your knees (cat). On the exhale, slide hands back to the thighs and arch your back and shoulders, chin slightly up to the sky (cow) and exhale loudly through the mouth (Repeat this seated cat/cow three times.
- Come back to a neutral position, close your eyes, and breathe slowly and evenly for three breaths. Notice how you feel.

Round 2

- Shoulder Rolls: Raise shoulders up to your ears and roll back and down, squeezing your shoulder blades together as best as you can. Do this three times, then raise and roll forward three times.
- Either sitting on a chair or on a mat, circle your hips clockwise three or four rounds, then counter clockwise.
- Place right ankle on left knee and gentle apply pressure to right thigh for three or four counts. Then do the opposite side (left ankle on right thigh).
- Come back to a neutral position, close your eyes, and breathe slowly and evenly for three breaths. Notice how you feel.

Round 3

- Tapping: With two fingers, gently tap your neck, throat, and chest area to stimulate your throat and heart chakra. Do this for about three or four rounds of breath.
- Come back to a neutral position, close your eyes, and breathe slowly and evenly for three breaths. Notice how you feel.

Step 2: Write

Reflect upon your first love. Or your first kiss. Or your first sexual experience. What do you remember? Try to write as many sensory details as you can. Take yourself back in time to relive your first...

Set your timer for 10 minutes and write:
"My first love... or *"The first time I thought I was in love..."*

Step 3: Transcribe and Share

When your timer goes off (or when you're finished writing) if you choose, you can transcribe whatever you wrote into a document on your computer. Maybe you want to craft this into a life story, or let it sit for a while and come back to it on another day.

Remember that you can join and share your writing in the private Facebook group Yogic Writing with Rebecca.

DAY 14

MOTHERS

There's a story behind everything. Sometimes the
stories are simple, and sometimes they are hard and
heartbreaking. But behind all your stories is your
mother's story, because hers is where yours begins.
—Mitch Albom*y*

A FEW YEARS AGO, I ATTENDED A BORN TO RISE™ WOMEN'S STORY
festival where my eighty-one-year-old mother was one of the speakers,
and she shared a story about her life. As a teenager she was quarantined
in a tuberculosis sanitarium for two years, and she talked about how
that experience left her with a never-ending positive outlook on life,
even amidst the most difficult times.

My mother recovered from her tuberculosis and was released from
the hospital at fifteen years old. Three years later a Greek marriage
was arranged, and a year after that, her first daughter was born. Two
more daughters followed and then a son. By the time she was twenty-
nine, she had four children under the age of ten.

Her marriage to my father lasted eighteen years. At the age of
thirty-six, they divorced and she lived out her lost teenage years. With
no financial support from my father, we lost our four-bedroom home
in a suburban family neighborhood and moved to a two-bedroom
apartment in a nearby city. My mother had to work outside the home
for the first time in her life, and discovered all that she never had as

a teenager. She went to her first concert, saw her first sunrise, dated much younger men, and got a few tatoos.

She always provided a roof over our head and food on the table (even if she wasn't there often to share a meal with us) but in many ways during this time of newfound freedom in my mother's life, my siblings and I were left on our own.

I've heard my mother's story many times, but this time I heard it in a different way. I understood, perhaps for the first time, exactly what Mitch Albom is saying; my mother's story is where my story begins.

My childhood was strongly impacted by my mother's early trauma, her life as a young mother, and her experiences during the 1970s when she was spreading her wings for the first time.

So when I heard from a friend who is trying to write a story about her mother's life and doesn't know where to start, I suggested, "Write *your* story. Write about the kind of mother she was. Write about your relationship when you were a child, and a teenager, and when you became a mother. Your mother's story will surface through yours."

I know a little something about that.

"Behind all your stories is your mother's story, because hers is where yours begins."

Step 1: Breathe

(Pranamaya kosha)

We begin our practice today with a breath practice called left-nostril breathing, or LNYB (left-nostril yogic breathing).

In yogic breathing practices, we pay attention to which nostril we are inhaling from because of the effects it can have on our nervous systems and which hemispheres of our brains are stimulated. Both ancient yogi science and modern science agree that there is a relationship between the left side of the body and the right hemisphere of the brain, as well as the right side of the body with the left hemisphere of our brain. In this breath practice, we are only going to breathe through the left nostril.

Simply speaking, according to ancient yogic philosophy, there are three energy channels (called nadis) in our body (left, center, and right). The left energy nadi is called the *ida* and is thought to be associated with feminine energy and the right side of the brain. When we breathe through the left nostril, we enhance the flow of prana (breath) through the *ida* energy channel, as well as stimulate the right side of our brain, which is associated with creativity. Breathing through the left nostril also activates our parasympathetic nervous system, which is responsible for the rest and digest response.

Left-Nostril Yoga Breathing Instructions:

- Sit tall and gently place your right thumb against the right nostril to close it. Point your other four fingers on your right hand up toward the sky.
- Inhale and exhale slowly through the left nostril, pausing briefly at the top of the breath.
- Exhale slowly through the left nostril, pausing at the end of the exhale.
- Practice this for three to five minutes. You can count the inhale and the exhale, with the intention to make the exhale one count longer than the inhale.
- When your timer goes off, release your right hand to rest in your lap, and experiment with doing this exercise without your thumb closing your right nostril. That is, think about breathing only through your left nostril. What do you notice?
- Return to your normal breath pattern and see if you can feel the effects of the LNYB. Do you feel calm and relaxed? Are you ready to write?

Step 2: Writing

Think about your relationship with your mother and how it may have changed throughout the years. Write about how it was when you were a child, teenager, or adult, or if and when you became a mother yourself. Explore what you may have inherited from your mother, either directly or indirectly through her life story.

Set your timer for ten minutes, and write one of these prompts.

"My mother and I are ..." or *"My mother and I were ..."*

Step 3: Transcribe and Share

When you're ready, transcribe whatever you wrote into a document on your computer. Read it with compassionate eyes (as if someone else wrote it) and see if there is a story there you want to expand upon.

Remember that you can also join and share your writing in the private Facebook group Yogic Writing with Rebecca.

DAY 15

SECRETS

> You own everything that happened to you. Tell
> your stories. If people wanted you to write warmly
> about them, they should have behaved better.
> —Anne Lamott

TODAY I AM GOING TO SUGGEST THAT YOU WRITE AS IF PUBLISHING your writing is not an option. Throw away the fear of so-and-so never speaking to you again. Forget about hurting someone's feelings. Forget about telling the secret you promised would stay safe with you.

Control can neuter writing. You can deal with control when it comes time to publish what you are writing, but *not* when you are in the process of writing!

I challenge you to just give it a try. Write down your truest feelings about something as if *no one* will ever—*ever*—read what you say. Tell yourself right now that you will shred everything on the paper you're writing on.

Instead of sharing what you wrote today, you can share the experience of how it felt. (Of course, you can also choose to share what you wrote, but the point is when you're writing it, you don't consider that an option.)

Shake things up.

Write with abandon.

Step 1: Balance Your Throat Chakra

To read more about the chakra system, refer to part 1, chapter 2.

According to ancient yogic scriptures, every person has a set of energy centers, called chakras, starting at the base of the spine and running upward to the crown of the head. The fifth chakra, known as the throat chakra, lies at the point of the throat or neck and is associated with creativity and communication. Its color is blue, and the sound associated with it is *hum*. People with balanced throat chakras can express themselves well, particularly verbally. It is important for you, as a writer, to keep your throat chakra open and balanced. Ways to balance your throat chakra are singing, humming, chanting *hummm*, and repeating positive affirmations to yourself.

- Sit up tall with a long spine and gently place one hand over your throat and one hand on your belly. Take a deep inhale, filling your belly all the way, and then exhale with the sound of *hummmmmm*. Do this three or four more times—deep inhale and *hummmmmmm* as you exhale.
- As you continue to repeat this mantra six or seven times, imagine your throat chakra opening and all blockages releasing and dissipating.
- Next, repeat this affirmation to yourself: *I speak and write my authentic truth, with confidence, clarity, and compassion.*

Step 2: Write

Of all the writing prompts I have ever shared or used myself, this one is the easiest—and the hardest. You can alternate between the two to see what is revealed. Remember you are writing today as if *no one* will ever read this.

Set your timer for ten minutes and write:

"What I can't write about is ..." or *"I've never told anyone ..."*

Step 3: Transcribe and Share

If you choose, you can transcribe whatever you wrote into a document on your computer and play with it. Or you can choose to rip it up and throw it in the trash, or even burn it. The fact that you wrote what you can't write about can be healing in and and of itself. Maybe you want to just let it sit and marinate just as it is. You can always come back to this raw writing on another day.

Remember that you can also join and share your writing or how you felt about this exercise in the private Facebook group Yogic Writing with Rebecca.

DAY 16

WRITING ABOUT
THE PANDEMIC

Life is what happens to you while
you're busy making other plans.
—John Lennon

THE UNDERSTATEMENT OF THE YEAR 2020, RIGHT?

Do you remember your New Year's resolution on January 1, 2020? How did you think that year would unfold? Did your house change from a place to come home to to a place you never left? Family celebrations, weddings, funerals ... all taking place on zoom. Sports events, concerts, conferences, all cancelled. Restaurants, stores and schools closed. No traffic on the streets and quiet airports. Masks became a required accessory. An election that seemed to never end. So many lives were lost.

And in the middle of *all* that—there was *you*.

One day, years from now, you will be asked about all of this. Your kids, grandkids, great-grandkids, and others will want to know. What will you say? What stories will you remember? What details will you forget?

Each one of us has a story of how the covid pandemic changed us. Don't let the historians be the only ones who tell the story. Write your story down. It matters.

Step 1: Meditate with your breath

(Manomaya kosha / Pranamaya kosha)

I believe there are misconceptions surrounding meditation, including that it must be done in a special way or that you must sit in a certain position or that you should try to not think about anything (as if that's possible). In my opinion, the key to meditation is not about trying to empty your mind, but instead developing a nonjudgmental awareness of sensations, feelings, and thoughts. Telling yourself not to think will only produce the opposite effect. But you can choose how to respond to those thoughts and then let them go and bring your awareness back to your breath.

You can also give your mind something to do, such as counting the breath, which helps it to not wander to other things. After a while, you might lose the counting and sit in silence.

1. Take a seat or lie down anywhere you're comfortable—on a chair, on your bed, on the floor. Set your timer for five minutes. Gently breathe in and out through your nose two or three times.

2. Now take a deeper breath in through your nose, expand your belly with a count of 1–2–3–4, pause for a few counts, and then exhale through your nose for a count of 1–2–3–4–5 and pause. Then repeat. Inhale through the nose for a count of four, pause exhale through the nose for a count of five, or even six. Keep it nice and slow. The key here is for your exhale to be one or two counts longer than your inhale.

When you find your mind drifting away to a thought about something, whatever it is, acknowledge that you are thinking by saying to yourself, *I am thinking,* and then go back to counting the breath.

Step 2: Write

Take a moment and think about all the things you remember about life during the covid 19 pandemic. How did your everyday life change? What about your job? Your social life? Your day-to-day activities? Did you move? Did family members move in with you? Did you have school children at home? Did you have to change plans for a vacation or event you had planned? Etc., etc., etc... Start by making a list or a brain dump of anything and everything you can remember with as much detail as possible.

Then choose one or two things on that list and expand.

"What I remember about 2020..."

Step 3: Transcribe and Share

Transcribe what you wrote into a document on your computer. Maybe you want to expand on a few of the things that you remembered and continue to craft this story as a part of your legacy to pass down to generations to come.

Remember that you can join and share your writing in the private Facebook group Yogic Writing with Rebecca.

DAY 17

THE MUNDANE

Every day of your life is a remarkably interesting
sequence of thoughts, feelings, memories, dreams,
events and interactions, worthy of writing down.
—Lesléa Newman

ARE YOU FEELING REMARKABLE? DO YOU LOOK AROUND AND SAY
to yourself "Wow, my life is extraordinary! I am *ah-mazing!*"

If you don't, you should.

Lesléa Newman, the author of *Heather Has Two Mommies* (the first
children's book addressing same sex parents, published in 1989—and
still in print today!) often writes about how every life is remarkable.

Even yours.

Especially yours.

Today I challenge you to write about all the boring, unremarkable,
ordinary things in your life. When you do that, I bet you will find that
there are some truly remarkable things hiding below the surface once
you start digging.

The ordinary will become extraordinary. Write about those
moments in your life.

Step 1: Daily Affirmations

(Vijnanamaya kosha)

Affirmations are a beautiful way to start the day and saying positive affirmations to yourself taps into your vijnanamaya kosha, your wisdom body. Just try it and see how it makes you feel.

Take a seat anywhere you're comfortable. Set your timer to five minutes. Gently breathe in and out through your nose two or three times. Then wrap your arms around yourself in a big hug.

Say something to yourself you might say to a child or someone you love. For example: *I love you. You are amazing. You are enough. You are worthy. You are lovable. You are blessed. You have everything you need within you.*

Continue to breathe in and out through the nose, while repeating these affirmations to yourself.

As Louise L. Hay, the founder of Hay House Publishing said, "You have been criticizing yourself for years, and it hasn't worked. Try approving of yourself and see what happens."

When you're ready, set your timer for ten minutes, and take out your journal and pen to write.

Step 2: Write

Today let's write about the mundane. First, you will write a list, and then pick one thing on the list to describe in full detail. This is great practice for writing life stories. They say that God is in the details, so remember to write as many as you can.

"Three things I do every day …"

Now pick one of those things and write, in detail, how you went about doing it. Write about that one thing for ten minutes, and see what happens. It might invoke a memory. It might invoke a feeling or emotion. It might invoke a desire or dream, or it might just be a detailed account of how you brush your teeth. It doesn't matter; just go with it. Whatever shows up is perfect, as long as there are details.

Step 3: Transcribe and Share

When your timer goes off (or when you're finished writing) if you choose, you can transcribe whatever you wrote into a document on your computer and begin to play with it. Maybe you want to expand on something that showed up.

Remember that you can also join and share your writing in the private Facebook group Yogic Writing with Rebecca.

DAY 18

HOME

Home is the nicest word there is.
—Laura Ingalls Wilder

WRITING ABOUT YOUR HOME (OR HOMES) FROM YOUR CHILDHOOD can be a very juicy topic to generate multiple life stories. You can write about your bedroom, for example, and that can bring up one kind of story. You can write about your house and your neighborhood, and that can bring up a whole slew of stories. Or, as in the case of military families, perhaps you lived in multiple childhood homes and what you need to write about is that experience. I know families that have lived in the same home passed down from one generation to the next, and other families (like mine) who moved every two or three years so nothing felt permanent.

Because memories are often associated with one or more of your senses, one way to jog your memory is to activate your senses. A song, or a smell, or a taste can bring you back to a scene and details suddenly become alive. Another way to jog your memory about your childhood home is to sketch a picture of it—either the floorplan of the home as you remember it, or one particular room (your bedroom, for example) and draw where the furniture was situated, any objects in the room, any pictures or posters on the wall, was it neat and tidy or were there clothes on the floor? Draw as many details as possible, and from there you can begin to write.

Step 1: Mindfulness through the Senses

(Vijnanamaya Kosha)

This mindfulness exercise involves isolating one sense at a time and paying attention to whatever comes into your awareness through that sense. It is a highly effective way to find your grounding and feel more centered. It is also a helpful exercise to do before you write. Adding sensory details in your writing makes it come alive.

Begin the exercise in a comfortable seat with your feet firmly planted on the ground. Take a few deep, slow breaths.

- Start by bringing your awareness to your sense of vision. With a soft gaze, bring your attention to any object in front of you as if it were the first time you saw it. Really look at it for at least ten or fifteen seconds. Then look up toward the ceiling, to your left and right, and down toward your feet, each time finding an object to pay close attention to—five different objects using your sense of sight.
- Now close your eyes and bring your attention to your sense of hearing. Take a breath or two to open yourself up to the sounds around you or even within your body. Try to find four different sounds to pay attention to.
- Next gently move your attention to your sense of taste. Sense the taste within your mouth, just as it is right now. Bring your attention to three different tastes, even if you have to imagine them.
- Then isolate your sense of smell and bring your awareness to it. You might smell something specific or something more neutral. Try to smell two different sensations, even if you imagine them, for ten to fifteen seconds each.
- Lastly, let your attention shift to the sense of touch. Pay attention to whatever sense of touch comes into your awareness—your body in contact with the floor or your chair,

your clothes against your skin, or you might even rub your fingertips against each other, and feel that sensation.

- To end the exercise, take a few deep breaths and open your eyes. Pay attention to how your whole body feels now, grounded and in tune with each of your five senses.

Step 2: Write

Think about your childhood home or homes. You can start this writing excersice by first drawing a sketch of your home or a particular room in it. Include as many details as possible.

How was your childhood home different than your home today.

Set your timer for ten minutes, and write down one of the following prompts.

"My home is ... or *"My home was ..."*

Keep your hand moving! Don't take the pen off the page for the entire ten minutes.

Step 3: Transcribe and Share

When your timer goes off (or when you're finished writing) if you choose, you can transcribe whatever you wrote into a document on your computer and begin to play with it. Maybe you want to expand on something that came out, or maybe you want to just let it sit and marinate just as it is. You can always come back to this raw writing on another day.

Remember that you can also join and share your writing in the private Facebook group Yogic Writing with Rebecca.

DAY 19

FATHERS

> I believe that we don't choose our stories.
> Our stories choose us. And if we don't tell
> them, then we are somehow diminished.
> —Dani Shapiro

DANI SHAPIRO HIT THE NAIL ON THE HEAD FOR ME WHEN SHE said, "Our stories choose us." I have been writing about my father for years and years and years. And believe me, it's not because I want to, but the guy just won't let me go.

In Facebook terms, my relationship with my father would be "it's complicated." We had some good years, and others—not so much. But in the end, we forgave each other for not being able to completely smooth out the rough edges of our relationship.

He died unexpectedly the day before my son was born. I was living in California, and he was in Rhode Island. His spirit came to me in my hospital room that same night looking young, happy, and healthy and gave me a kiss on my forehead. He then bent over to kiss my son, sleeping in the bassinet beside me.

All of my father stories reside at the cellular level, and every time I think I'm *done* writing about him and what he taught me—both through his presence and his absence—one more sneaky little story makes it way to the surface.

And so I take a breath, and I write.

Step 1: Breathe

(Pranamaya Kosha)

This breath practice is called *Kapalabhatti*, and is used to awaken energy and focus. *Kapala* in Sanskrit translates to *skull* and *bhati* means light. So when you are practicing this exercise, think of a bright light entering your skull to wake you up!

(Do not practice kapalabhati if you are pregnant or if you have high blood pressure, acid gastric issues, heart disease, abdominal pain, or if it makes you feel dizzy. It's always best to start slowly, and then with time you can increase the speed and number of rounds.)

To practice kapalabhati breath:

1. Sit comfortably in an upright position and place your hands on your lower belly. If you're sitting in a chair, make sure to have both feet on the ground. Start by first noticing your regular inhale and exhale. Stay with that for a few breaths. Then think about lifting the crown of your head toward the heavens, feeling a lift to your body and the back of your spine.

2. Take a deep, cleansing breath in through your nose and out through your mouth.

3. Now inhale again through your nose, filling your belly with air about halfway full.

4. Forcefully expel all the air from your lungs through your nose in short spurts while drawing your navel in toward your spine. Don't worry about the inhalation; it will happen naturally. Take ten to twenty forceful exhale breaths like this to complete one round.

5. After completing the round, relax with your eyes closed and observe the sensations in your body. Then allow your breathing to return to normal, and if you choose you can begin another round. The count and rounds can be increased gradually over time, but don't do more than three rounds of ten as a beginner.

Step 2: Write

Think about your father or another father-like figure you've had in your life. Feel free to write about either the man himself or your relationship with him or any scene you remember with the two of you together. Just see what's there.

"My father is (or was) ..." or *"My father taught me ..."*

Step 3: Transcribe and Share

When your timer goes off (or when you're finished writing) if you choose, you can transcribe whatever you wrote into a document on your computer. Maybe you want to expand on something that came out, or maybe you want to just let it sit and marinate just as it is. You can always come back to this raw writing on another day.

Remember that you can also join and share your writing in the private Facebook group Yogic Writing with Rebecca.

DAY 20

GRATITUDE

When you undervalue what you do, the
world will undervalue who you are.
—Oprah Winfrey

HAVE YOU EVER KEPT A GRATITUDE JOURNAL OR MADE A LIST OF all the things you are grateful for? More and more research has shown the positive effects of expressing gratitude can have on your life and relationships, as well as your mental and physical health. Just a few minutes a day can make a huge impact on your perspective on life.

Typically, when we think about what we are grateful for, the same things show up, like health, family, home, pets, job, and so forth. And while those things are absolutely worthy of gratitude, I feel like sometimes we could dig a little deeper and think about the little things that may go unnoticed that are also worthy of gratitude.

Think about this? When is the last time you expressed gratitude for *yourself*?

We have been talking and thinking about the layers of our being, our koshas, through which we experience our world. Now as we near the last day of this twenty-one-day journey, take a moment and express gratitude for each of these layers that make up who you are.

Step 1: Gratitude Mantra Meditation - Kritajna Hum (kree-tah-jna-hum)

(Manomaya kosha)

The meaning of this mantra is: *I am gratitude.* It cultivates self-awareness and allows us to accept that we are thankful.

As you inhale deeply, say the first part of the mantra to yourself: *kree-tah-jna*. Pause for a second, and then say *hum* with a long exhale, dropping your shoulders and releasing your jaw.

Inhale *kree-Tah-Jna* (pause), exhale *hum* (pause). Repeat the mantra with your breath ten times or for five minutes. When you're ready, pick up your journal and pen… and once again, smile!

Step 2: Write

Instead of thinking about what or who you are grateful for today, I ask that you give *yourself* a great big gratitude hug.

You are here. You are alive. Your physical body allows you to move. Your emotional body allows you to think and feel. Your energetic body allows you to breathe! Your wisdom body allows you to honor your intuition, and your spiritual body allows you to have faith and be in touch with your bliss.

Now take out your journal and write, *"I am grateful for today."*

Set your timer for ten minutes and first say out loud the following mantras, and then write them down.

"I am grateful for my body."
"I am grateful for my breath."
"I am grateful for my mind."
"I am grateful for my intuition."
"I am grateful for my spirit."

111

Now choose any one of those and write more about it. Why are you grateful for your body? When was a time in your life you were particularly grateful for your body, your mind, your intuition, or your spirit (perhaps your faith?)

Step 3: Transcribe and Share

When your timer goes off (or when you're finished writing) if you choose, you can transcribe whatever you wrote into a document on your computer and begin to play with it. Maybe you want to expand on something that came out and begin to craft a story from it.

Remember that you can also join and share your writing in the private Facebook group Yogic Writing with Rebecca.

IF ONLY I HAD KNOWN

*Writing is like driving at night. You can see only as far as
the headlights, but you can make the whole trip that way.*
—E. L. Doctorow

WHETHER YOU WROTE ONE DAY OR EVERY DAY, FOR TEN MINUTES
or more; whether you meditated or practiced a new way of breathing;
whether you transcribed, edited, or shared your work, or some
combination of the above, one thing is for sure: *You did it.* You should
be proud of *yourself*!

You picked up your pen or tapped on your keyboard for five, ten,
or twenty-one days, and you went *inward* and found a piece of you that
had been hiding, patiently waiting for you to come and get it.

And that's exactly what you did. No one did it for you. It was
all you.

You picked up your pen, you met your resistance, and then you
let it go.

So now that you know how it feels to take ten or fifteen minutes
to meditate and breathe, to reflect, write, and share, are you going to
continue to do so?

Step 1: Yoga

(Anamaya kosha)

In my personal story of how yoga changed my life and my writing, I introduced you to my teacher and mentor, Devarshi Steven Hartman. He's a total kick in the pants, and he's more skilled at yoga than anyone I know. And I don't mean stand-on-your-head skilled (though he does that), but rather the way he embodies and teaches yoga to anyone and everyone regardless of physical or mental limitations is truly astounding.

Devarshi has several recorded videos on his YouTube channel, and I encourage you to find a practice and give it a try. There is an introduction to yoga practice, along with some ten-minute shoulder and neck stretching, breath practices, and a full prannothan yoga practice. Go to YouTube and search for Devarshi Stephen Hartman, and pick a practice!

Give it a try! And then when you're done, just sit quietly for a moment and see how you feel.

Step 2: Write

Take a moment and reflect upon everything you've been writing about these past twenty-one days. A lot of has surfaced. And yet, there is so much more to say.

Set your timer for ten minutes, and write down these words: *"If only I had known…"*

If nothing comes to mind, keep writing the prompt.

If only I had known … If only I had known … If only I had known …

Step 3: Transcribe and Share

When your timer goes off (or when you're finished writing) if you choose, you can transcribe whatever you wrote into a document on your computer. Or maybe you just want to reflect on this piece. This is one you can come back to again and again.

Remember that you can also join and share your writing in the private Facebook group Yogic Writing with Rebecca.

Don't forget the most important part!
Thank yourself for showing up!

DAY 22

WAIT, WHAT?

"Why bother? Because right now there is someone
out there with a wound in the exact shape of
your words." —Sean Thomas Dougherty

FOR ME, WRITING IS A SPIRITUAL PRACTICE. IT IS HOW I CONNECT
to my higher power on a daily basis. Sometimes I ask questions,
sometimes answers are revealed. Sometimes I write what I don't want
anyone else to read. Sometimes I write and something shows up that
I want the entire world to read! Sometimes I feel like I'm moving
my pen, and sometimes my pen is moving me. I never know what to
expect, and much like yoga, every practice is different. The challenge,
for me, is to not be attached to the outcome. Easy to say, but not so
easy to do.

But there's one thing I know for sure, to quote Gloria Steinem,
"Writing is the only thing that when I do it, I don't feel I should be
doing something else."

What about you? Did this writing practice change anything
for you?

Did it allow you to listen to a voice that maybe you've been
ignoring for some time? Did it help you put things in perspective,
maybe see things in a different way?

If it did, great.

If it didn't, that's OK too. You've got plenty of time.

Writing improves with practice, and writing on a daily basis means a lot of practice. When you write every day, you train your brain to think faster and more efficiently, allowing you to put out better writing more frequently.

Remember the first day when you wrote, "I am a writer"?

Are you starting to believe that now?

Write your stories. No one else can do that but you. And above anything else, honor your story, even the hard parts. Especially the hard parts.

We write to heal. We write to reveal. We write to leave our legacy.

Thank you for taking this journey with me. I look forward to reading your stories!

Printed in the United States
by Baker & Taylor Publisher Services